My Best Screenplay

Straw Man

As I contemplated my lack of results with my pitches to producers and directors in the film industry, I had set my screenplays aside. But being a certified teacher of Business English, my goal is to now provide:

a well priced example for students of film writing -

and possible perusal by industry professionals.

Cover design by Lonnie P. Pelletier

Pelletier, Lonnie, 1943, author of the screenplay as an

adaptation of the book:

Memory Search also by Lonnie Pelletier

Title: My Best Musical Play / Lonnie Paul Pelletier

Includes bibliographical references

ISBN 978-1-928151-21-0

Subjects: Screenplay

STRAW MAN

Screenplay

by

Lonnie Pelletier

Adaptation from the novel

MEMORY SEARCH

by

Lonnie Pelletier

7328 Arcola Street

Burnaby, BC, V5E 0A7

Phone: 604-209-3926

Email: Lon@LonPelletier.com

"STRAW MAN"

FADE IN:

INT. SINGLE HOUSEKEEPING ROOM - NIGHT
CHARACTER #1
TONY AS A BOY, TONY AS A YOUNG MAN AND TONY IN HIS LATE
FIFTIES. HE HAS DARK HAIR, IS GOOD LOOKING AND IN ATHLETIC
CONDITION. HIS MANNERS ARE OF SOMEONE WELL LIKED AND
PRESENTABLE.
CHARACTER #2
EMILE, TONY'S FATHER IS MUCH LIKE TONY IN HIS LATE FIFTIES,
IN BOTH PHYSICAL LOOK AND PRESENTATION.

The small baby-faced boy the age of finishing grade three is
sitting on the single bed, showing himself to be vulnerable.
It is a large room, furnished with one chair, a three-quarter
sized bed and a hotplate for cooking. The radio is playing in
the corner. "Hey now buckaroos, here's a song we haven't
heard for awhile - at least fur two days: SQUAWS ALONG THE
YUKON ARE GOOD ENOUGH FOR ME."

                    EMILE
               (Arriving in the doorway)
          Hi Tony, I finally got into town to
          come and visit!

Tony gives a wide smile, saying nothing.

                    EMILE (CONT'D)
          How are you? Ca va? I just got back
          from the construction camp. Ca va?

                    TONY
          Okay.

                    EMILE
          What are you reading?

                    TONY
          Tom Sawyer

                    EMILE
          Do you know how it's going to end
          yet? I always want to know how they
          end.

                    TONY
          I know how it ends. I've read it
          twice before.

                    EMILE
          What? Why twice before? Is it your
          favorite?

                    TONY
          It's the only book that I've got,
          Dad.

Showing shock, EMILE comes over and sits on the bed with
TONY. He looks around the room to observe the lack of cooking
facilities.

                    EMILE
          What's the story about, son?

                    TONY
          It's about a boy my age. It's that
          the story could go on until the boy
          meets a girl. Her name was Becky.

                    EMILE
          Why son? Why does it end that way?

                    TONY
          Then, he has become a man. Life
          needs to begin another story then.

                    EMILE
               (Looking around with tears
                forming)
          Have you ever just climbed a tree
          in a back yard? Do you ever want
          to?

TONY smiles politely.

                    TONY
          We've been moving around a lot,
          Dad.

                    EMILE
          Promise me one thing, Tony. Do you
          promise to one day find a Becky? - -
          I now know things about Buzz and
          your uh, surroundings that I never
          knew before - - things that can't
          be changed. Will you truly promise
          to one-day find a Becky?

                    TONY
          I promise, Dad.

EMILE walks across the room slowly, and exits and closes the door behind him. TONY looks at the closed door with silent resignation.

                                        DISSOLVE TO:

INT. A SMALL TOWN GENERAL STORE - NIGHT
CHARACTER #3:
JEAN, IN GRADE ELEVEN, SPORTING NINETEEN-FIFTIES STYLES, IS A
SLIM RED-HEAD, CUTE WITH BOBBY SOCKS, LOOSE SWEATER AND HAIR
SLICKED BACK. SHE IS THREE YEARS OLDER THAN TONY.

                    JEAN
          Hi, Tony. This is cool. I'm glad
          you could make it. This important
          thing happened today.

TONY is dressed entirely in black, nonchalant, greasy hair
combed back into a duck-tail, and attempting to be cool by
posture, as a tough-guy approach to the social scene. He is
in grade-eight but his eyes are dead and his sneer is set.

                    TONY
          Yeh, like what could be important
          today?

                    JEAN
          This guy that everyone is talking
          about just was killed. His name is
          James Dean. He's like a star. He's
          the ultimate teenager.

                    TONY
          Why? Is that important?

                    JEAN
          It is when you want to be cool!
          It's not like our queer parents,
          Tony. Like they want us to look up
          to your parent's homosexual
          friends.

                    TONY
          Yeh. Like my mother's best friend
          Maggie. She's still trying to get
          me to wear a dress.

                    JEAN
          I think that they've given up on
          you Tony. I came along... Well, I
          guess my Mom is just as bad. She's
          a dyke too... Look Tony.
                    (MORE)

> JEAN (CONT'D)
> Here is a photo of James Dean in
> this magazine.

The teenage group assembles with them around the magazine and
then breaks up into couples for their separate strolls home.

> CUT TO:

INT. LIVING ROOM OF TYPICAL MID-WEST HOUSE - NIGHT
CHARACTER #4:
ANNE IS BRUNETTE, A YOUNG WOMAN OF ABOUT TWENTY AND LATER IN
HER FORTIES. SHE IS TONY'S COUNTERPART IN LOOKS AND
PRESENTATION. HER CHARACTER TOGGLES BETWEEN THAT OF A CHURCH
LADY AND A SEEMINGLY COOL TEENAGER DUE TO MULTIPLE
PERSONALITIES.
CHARACTER #5:
JAKE, ANNE'S FATHER IS SHORT, STERN AND OUT OF STYLE, WITH
GRAY HAIR.
CHARACTER #6:
ANNE'S MOTHER. STERN AND LACKING CONFIDENCE. SHE IS A BEATEN
WOMAN IN ALL ASPECTS.
CHARACTER #7:
THE COUNTRY PASTOR, STERN AND CONFIDENT.

ANNE, and ANNE'S MOTHER are sitting on a couch and JAKE is
sitting on an easy-chair.

> ANNE
> Mom, Dad, I have something to tell
> you... I've been with Tony and I've
> made a decision... We need to talk
> about sex. I know that you like
> Robert best. He's a fundamentalist,
> but Robert is also a homosexual.

JAKE jumps up yelling.

> JAKE
> I'll see about this! And where do
> you get the idea that homosexuals
> even exist? The birds and the bees
> are about what you have in your
> tummy. That's all it is. The baby
> is God's will! Now go to your room
> and I'll call the pastor. Go to
> your room and pray to God and
> repent!

> ANNE
> No. We can talk about this!

JAKE grabs ANNE by her arm and drags her towards her bedroom.
She struggles against him as he forces her up the stairs.

Once in her room, she turns and sobs, collapsing on her bed. She later hears THE PASTOR talking along with others arriving. ANNE'S MOTHER knocks, enters and motions her to come downstairs. She then joins THE PASTOR in the living room and her parents stay in the kitchen with the others.

> THE PASTOR
> The husband must have authoritative power over his wife, and the father authoritative power over his children. Eve was formed from the rib of Adam and she was man's necessary companion and a useful person when kept in her place. The daughter's role is to never be defiant of her father's wishes. It is well written in Old Testament Scriptures... Man is rational and woman is emotional, Anne is now only being emotional... Man's reason must rule over this affliction. An adulteress perverts love into lust and ruins the family. She can subvert order. Anne needs to be careful of the wrath of God...

THE PASTOR turns away from the others listening in the kitchen and now is focused on ANNE.

> PASTOR
> Anne, do you understand that you must believe in biblical text where generations to follow, the sinning ancestors, are dealt with by God?

> ANNE
> Yes - of course, Pastor.

ANNE looks up timidly.

> PASTOR
> You have let the devil's ways into your life and your baby will rot in hell. Your baby will be tormented into eternity! - Are you frightened?

> ANNE
> Yes, yes I am.

                  PASTOR
You are sitting before the judgment
and wrath of God himself. Are you
really frightened?

                  ANNE
Yes, yes, yes.

                  PASTOR
Now you know God. Do you know God?

                  ANNE
Yes. Yes, I do.

                  PASTOR
Will you obey your father?

                  ANNE
Yes, yes.

                  PASTOR
Do you understand the reason for
obeying your father?

                  ANNE
Yes. It is the will of God.

MR. AND MRS. DAVIS, her future mother and father-in-law enter
the room, from the kitchen. ANNE turns to them.

                  ANNE (CONT'D)
I beg forgiveness. I pray for
repentance. I am his servant.

                  PASTOR
God, give us your redeeming grace
in accepting this wretched child
back to your comforting arms, back
to her family and away from the
control by the ways of the devil.
Amen.

They all hug.

                  ANNE
                  (Looking away briefly)
Tony will understand, I know he
will.

                            DISSOLVE TO:

EXT. A SMALL LAKE, ROLLING HILLS IN THE BACKGROUND - DAY

ANNE is sitting in a small rowboat talking to TONY. He is
slowly rowing.

>   ANNE
>   Things could only have happened as
>   they had, if God had planned it.
>   Tony, you'll go on to be extremely
>   successful - and both Robert and I
>   will have university degrees. My
>   pastor has guaranteed it. We'll be
>   seeing you in the elite and
>   successful cliques, as all three of
>   us are to now excel into the
>   future. What I really love is the
>   intensity. It's the church's laying
>   on of hands by my parents and my
>   pastor. It's like an exorcism! The
>   chants, and choruses are beautiful,
>   Tony.

>   TONY
>   We just made love! What...

                                        CUT TO:

EXT. WHEAT FIELD - DAY
CHARACTER #8:
BILL, TWENTY-ONE, THE SAME AGE AS TONY. A FARM BOY, HE DRIVES
A TRUCK FOR A LIVING.

On a summer's day, TONY walks into the center of the wheat
field on the edge of town, immediately adjacent to a new home
subdivision. He holds his arms out, like a scarecrow and
turns slowly. He is talking to himself as BILL joins him.

>   TONY
>   I was just dumped by Anne, my
>   girlfriend of five years. Anne and
>   her family were religious
>   fundamentalists - so, I'm standing
>   here.

>   BILL
>   I didn't want to interrupt you,
>   Tony. I thought that you might be
>   praying. I often used to walk into
>   the open field on my parents' farm
>   to do the same thing.

                    TONY
No, I was just thinking. I was
contemplating life while standing
away from all of the buildings.
Remember Anne?

                    BILL
I thought that you two would be
married by now.

                    TONY
Well, my perception of life had
once been that people shouldn't get
married until they were about
twenty-four. Maybe that was my
problem. I told her last Christmas,
when she received a mink stole from
her parents that it was clear that
it was more than just a symbol of
her becoming a confirmed adult
member of her church. I said that
she was now bought and paid for.
She claimed that she didn't
understand... We broke up, then
later we went together.

                    BILL
You've been through the mill.

                    TONY
Man, we broke up eight times. After
that she helped me celebrate my
twenty-first birthday with sex. She
used to compare me to Hemingway.
She often really believed that I
would be better off challenging my
world without her. At the spring
break, she was teaching so she
phoned as soon as she arrived in
town. We had sex... We snuck it…
throughout the spring break. It
didn't make sense... Then I
received a phone call message just
before the May 24th weekend. It was
to meet Anne at the Pine Lake
Cabins. We talked about Robert, the
supposed perfect fundamentalist and
the marriage choice of her parents.
He's a homosexual...

                    BILL
I'm now also convinced that there
are homosexuals, Tony.

                    TONY
Yeh, well, man, I carried Anne
across the cabin's threshold, like
I'll never bother to go through
that again. We spent three days
there. And then Anne told me she
was pregnant. Anne had become
engaged to Robert, the homosexual
had now been coupled, and everyone
within his little circle was happy.
We had rented a boat to go out on
the lake and all she could talk
about was her and Robert being part
of God's Plan. None of it made
sense.

                    BILL
Wow. That really is something. I
kept running into you guys when you
were together. Wow.

                    TONY
I had worked for Jake, for Anne's
ass-hole of a father during grades
eleven and twelve, at the Drilling
Mud warehouse.

                    BILL
Actually, when I saw you out here,
I watched you for a while, and I
was concerned whether you might
kill yourself.

                    TONY
No, I'm going to Europe. It's a
future and life to look forward to.
But, how about an educated opinion?
Does this fundamentalist group make
sense? I couldn't even go to their
church if I wanted to.

                    BILL
Naw, I can bring anyone that would
want to attend to my church.
Anyway, I believe in a Journey to
Faith rather than instant religion.
You have to study for it. So you
and Anne could be together.
Somehow, the Thomson family isn't
involved in normal
fundamentalism... Even as a Baptist
I really enjoyed your high school
jokes. Good luck to you, Tony.

They then shake hands and part, waving in the distance.

CUT TO:

EXT. OUTSIDE A DANCE HALL - NIGHT

CHARACTER #9:

GLORIA, TWENTY-THREE, A WELL-ENDOWED SWEATER-GIRL, SHE HAS LONG BRUNETTE HAIR AND IS AN EXTROVERT.

TONY is parked at the curb, in front of the dance hall at a lake. GLORIA jumps into Tony's car unannounced.

> GLORIA
>
> Hi, Tony. Can you give me a ride home?

> TONY
>
> Hey, where is Wayne? You guys have gone together forever.

> GLORIA
>
> No. We broke up forever ago. I'm working in the city now.

DISSOLVE TO:

INT. INSIDE TONY'S CAR PARKING IN THE MOONLIGHT - LATER

> GLORIA
>
> You know, Tony, I never really got to get to know you. What has your life been like?

> TONY
>
> Do you really want a summary?

> GLORIA
>
> Somehow, you're different. Like you talk about things.

> TONY
>
> Well, my parents separated when I was six. My father died when I had just turned twelve. I changed schools eleven times by the time I was eleven. My mother lined me up with a homosexual friend of hers when I was twelve. And the rest is easy stuff.

> GLORIA
>
> How old are you?

                    TONY
One year younger than you - but
I've matured a lot.

                    GLORIA
I did have a crush on you from a
distance, when I was in high
school, but I presumed that you
were over two years younger. What
ever happened to Anne? You and her
were quite an item.

                    TONY
I wasn't good enough for her
family. They broke us up. They're
religious fundamentalists...
Fanatics actually.

                    GLORIA
Really? It shouldn't have been a
problem. We used to go to their
church. You know I'm supposed to be
married by the time I've turned
twenty-four. I'm almost twenty-
three. Their belief is that
premarital sex will occur
otherwise. Funny, isn't it? Like
we're all virgins! And of course
there's the stigma of being
considered an old maid on a twenty-
fourth birthday.

                    TONY
How about a date for next Friday?
We need to spend some time
together.

                    GLORIA
Great! I'll come up from the city
and we can meet at the lake dance.
You can give me a ride home to my
parent's house after.

                    TONY
That's just the date that a guy
needs.

                                        DISSOLVE TO:

INT. NEW RESTAURANT - NIGHT

TONY and GLORIA are seated in a candle-lit setting. Soft
sixties music is playing in the background.

               GLORIA
    Hey, Tony. We've talked about
    relationships, even goals, and
    aspirations. You really can discuss
    things. It's like we've known each
    other forever... This is really a
    classy meal. You have a new flair
    for trying sophistication. Thanks.

               TONY
    Hey, you've made me feel human
    again. That was some rejection I
    just came through. I'm glad we
    decided to dine at Humber's Lodge.
    I know them. They're nice people.

               GLORIA
    My other dates must have worked at
    being farmers. They would make fun
    of eating at a restaurant with a
    tablecloth. I enjoyed you showing
    off your learned experience as a
    dashing young man about town.
    You're the kid from the shack on
    the edge of any town that you've
    lived-in. I enjoy every moment of
    this.

               TONY
    You definitely came at the right
    time.

               GLORIA
     (laughing)
    For you, Tony, I'll always cum at
    the right time!

                         DISSOLVE TO:

INT. INSIDE TONY'S CAR AS THE ACT OF SEX IS FLASHED - NIGHT -
ESTABLISHING

EXT. IN FRONT OF A NEWER HOME - LATER

TONY drops GLORIA off at her parent's house. The windows are
down. She speaks after she shuts the door of the car.

                    GLORIA
          Go get 'em, Tiger!

                    TONY
              (shouting back)
          I'll never forget you, Gloria!
          Anywhere I travel!

Tony has driven a few blocks, he is by himself.

                    TONY (CONT'D)
          You saved my life, Gloria. You're
          not Anne, but you saved my life.
          Now I can go to Europe! That's
          where I'll finally get love right!

                                        CUT TO:

EXT. A SIDE-WALK CAFE IN PARIS, FRANCE (1965) - NIGHT
CHARACTER #10:
INGRID IS FROM GERMANY AND IS A STUDENT IN PARIS. HOWEVER,
BEING IN HER YOUNG TWENTIES SHE IS SEXY AS A EUROPEAN WOMAN
AND SHE PRESENTS HERSELF AS BEING VERY WORLDLY. SHE IS
BRUNETTE AND WEARS FITTING CLOTHES FOR HER IDEAL FIGURE.

TONY and INGRID approach a group their age, obviously
friends. The group is a mix of German, Swedish and English
students. TONY is dressed in a turtle-neck sweater, the
others are dressed accordingly.

                    TONY
          Hi guys. Glad we caught you here.
          Ingrid and I just found a place
          together. It's a hotel just a few
          blocks from here. How's that for
          Parisian sixties style. Not bad for
          meeting just last weekend, eh?

                    GERMAN BLOND GIRL #1
          Ingrid, you work fast. You didn't
          even let the guy come up for air!

                    INGRID
          We both knew what we wanted. You're
          just too slow. And he did come up
          for air, often.

They laugh at a joke not truly understood by TONY.

                    GERMAN GIRL #2
          So you guys, are you still studying
          art history and at the Alliance
          Française together?

                    TONY
          Hey, we might go to Germany for a
          trip. I get to experience the real
          Europe. We'll definitely enjoy
          Paris together.

                    INGRID
          And I'll make sure that Tony has no
          more memories of the other side of
          the pond, by the time I get through
          with him.

They all laugh and make motions of a toast, not laughing at a
great joke, but at the sense of enjoying life.

                              DISSOLVE TO:

INT. STRIP CLUB IN FRANKFURT GERMANY (1965) - NIGHT

INGRID hands TONY a roll of bills, mostly American. He looks
at them in disgust, but with hesitation puts them into his
pocket.

                    TONY:
          I guess we didn't have to worry
          about running out of money.

                    INGRID
          No, Tony. But you need to relax
          more. Have fun. In a month or so
          you can decide what you want to do.
          You can work here in Germany - or
          not. Your choice... Have fun, after
          all I'm just a bar-girl... I'm not
          a whore. I get paid the big bucks
          for just talking to strangers.

                    TONY
          That's a lot of money per night. I
          just can't come to grips with it.
          It's like I'm pimping. We're now
          living at this expensive hotel.
          From what?

                    INGRID
          Relax Tony, this is what I did all
          through college. I've done it for
          at least six years. Think of me as
          back in Paris and as the college
          girl you knew. We have the same
          kind of perverted kid's background
          you know.

                    TONY
          I came to Europe to change my
          background - that's what's wrong
          with this. I actually wanted
          culture.

                    INGRID
          You get to drink at any bar uptown.
          You just walk in without a cover
          charge. They know us. You know you
          worry too much.

                    TONY
          I was asked twice last night by
          other girls if I wanted them to be
          my girl friend with their cash
          flow. That's with or instead of
          you. That doesn't seem like bar-
          girls. You're telling me that you
          get paid for enticing men to drink
          more. I'm telling you it doesn't
          make sense. You're making too much
          money.

                                        DISSOLVE TO:

INT. NOISY FRANKFURT TRAIN STATION - THE NEXT DAY

INGRID is saying good-bye to TONY with a hug.

                    INGRID
          Are you sure you don't want more
          money to take with you? You don't
          know how expensive Rome is.

                    TONY
          No, I have what I left Paris with.
          I'll chalk up the expensive dinners
          and the hotel as your hospitality.
          I really care for you Ingrid. It's
          been a great five months now.

                    INGRID
          Here's two sandwiches and a coke
          for overnight on the train.

                    TONY
          Thanks, Ingrid. You are able to
          take care of me like a wife. I
          guess you've said goodbye before.

                    INGRID
          You just couldn't figure out what
          you wanted from me.

                    TONY
          I'll write when I land somewhere
          and find a job... Probably in the
          south of France. Maybe I'll go to
          England. I can hitchhike anywhere.

                    INGRID
          Write me, Tony. Just send it in
          care of the bar. You know that I
          move a lot. I hope you find a home.

They kiss, hug, and part. TONY boards the worker's train to
Italy, he looks out the window. The sound of the Second World
War song AUF WIEDERSEHEN TILL WE MEET AGAIN seems to be
playing in the background.

                                        CUT TO:

INT. CANADIAN FAST FOOD RESTAURANT - DAY
CHARACTER #11:
GEORGE, A GOOD FRIEND OF TONY'S FROM HIGH SCHOOL. THEY ARE
MID-TWENTIES AND BOTH RATHER GOOD LOOKING AS COOL GUYS FOR
THE AGE. THEY ARE CLEAN CUT SIMILAR TO MOST COLLEGE STUDENTS.
CHARACTER #12
ROBERT ANNE'S NEW HUSBAND, IS A FEW YEARS BEHIND STYLE WITH A
BRUSH-CUT AND WESTERN STYLE SHIRT.

TONY and GEORGE enter for a snack and discovered that ANNE
and ROBERT are sitting at a booth near the door.

TONY waves as nonchalantly as possible and proceeds to order
and choose a booth on the opposite side of the restaurant.
Having personally achieved an air of what he considered
adequate non-commitment, he goes over to greet the couple.

                    TONY
          I just wanted to say hello and to
          congratulate you on your marriage,
          and of course wish you well.

                    ANNE
          Thank you, Tony. Of course you know
          Robert from years ago in high
          school.

                    ROBERT
          I got the girl.

                    TONY
          Do you think it was a soccer game?

                    ROBERT
          I know who you are, and I got the
          girl.

                    ANNE
          Was it like a soccer game? Was I
          supposed to be the prize?

                    ROBERT
          Okay, so no, it wasn't like a
          soccer game. There just isn't any
          reason to talk to rabble like this.

                    TONY
          Well, I would like to give you both
          my best wishes, and wish you great
          luck in the future.

TONY leans over to ROBERT'S right ear and speaks firmly.

                    TONY (CONT'D)
          Robert, go fuck yourself.

ROBERT immediately turns completely white-faced and sits
frozen. TONY smiles, nods politely to ANNE and then leaves to
join GEORGE.

                    GEORGE
          So... Do you still love her as much
          as you used to?

                    TONY
          I GUESS I'm slowly healing. Lets
          vow to lay off small town girls. If
          they haven't moved to the city, we
          won't go near them.

                    GEORGE
          You got that exactly right!

                                        CUT TO:

INT. LOBBY OF SMALL TOWN HOTEL - NIGHT

TONY dressed in a three-piece suit, enters the lobby of the
hotel. He finds himself face to face with ROBERT, ANNE,
ANNE'S MOTHER and her father JAKE. It is the mid-sixties.

                    JAKE
          Well, there's a face we haven't
          seen around here for awhile. How
          are you doin', my boy?

                    TONY
          Hello... Well, I was in Europe for
          a while.

                    JAKE
          We were just taking the youngsters
          out for their anniversary meal.
          Robert here is taking
          Engineering... Well now, as far as
          you, I guess you could use some
          work. I can't give you steady work,
          but I can give you some piecemeal
          hourly stuff. Are you still able to
          hack unloading those boxcars?

                    TONY
          Just a minute. Do you realize that
          I was studying in Paris?

                    JAKE
          Oh sure, I've been in touch with
          Buzz, your step-dad. Anyway, we
          were dining out today, which we
          often do as we like to celebrate
          the achievements of our young ones.
          Just call me sometime if you want
          to unload drilling mud.

                    TONY
          Let's get one thing straight. I
          offered my life for this family. I
          was willing to set aside any goals
          that I may have had. What you don't
          get to do is be condescending and
          infer that I am still just a
          labourer. My goal was to be an
          executive in the world of commerce
          and I have definitely achieved that
          goal.

                    JAKE
          Actually, I didn't want to say it,
          but it was more about you never
          going to church.

                    TONY
          Through my studies, I've been in
          more churches in Europe than you
          will ever probably be in. Let me be
          specific. Your reason for using the
          church was specifically for
          control. You've never cared about
          consequences to others. You're only
          concerned with your own personal
          control... You're a complete ass-
          hole.

ROBERT exits to stand outside to wait. He is wearing shorts
with a sweater tied around his waist giving a little boy
look.

                    JAKE
          Well, my boy, I have certain duties
          as the father of a young woman such
          as Anne here.

                    TONY
          I am not your boy. Rather, I am an
          adult in an adult world and that is
          the reason you didn't want me
          around. You wanted Anne to marry a
          boy-child so that you could control
          him too. I wouldn't fit that
          picture. That's my new car outside
          and I've been a leader in the
          industry of real estate sales for
          almost a year. Mrs. Thomson, if
          your husband ever beats you again,
          as he used to do, just phone me.
          I'm in the Calgary phone book. Good
          luck also, with having such a
          useless wimp for a son-in-law.
          Anne, I wish you well in life, and
          of course I wish you the best.

                    ANNE
          I wish you well and all the best
          also, Tony. I want you to know that
          my pregnancy was unsuccessful but
          I'm now pregnant again and
          attempting to have another. I
          really wish you well.

ROBERT rushes in from standing outside. He is out of breath.

                    ROBERT
          The police have just driven by.
          Should I go and shout for them,
          Dad? I can catch up to them on the
          other side of the block.

                    TONY
          Anne and I know every policeman
          well. We even worked with them
          through Teen Town. I don't think
          you'll get any help from them in
          stopping my communication here.

JAKE holds out his hand to TONY offering a handshake.

                    JAKE
          Sir, I wish you well in every
          endeavour that you might undertake.
          I give you my utmost respect.

                    TONY
          Don't be an idiot and don't
          patronize me. You've already
          screwed up more than enough lives.

TONY looks slowly at each member, as they stand seeming
helpless. He smiles and nods at MRS. THOMSON and ANNE
separately. He then walks off to the right towards the
hallway to the bar, and the men's washroom.

                              DISSOLVE TO:

INT. MEN'S WASHROOM, SMALL HOTEL - MOMENTS LATER

TONY is standing before the sink in the men's room as if
frozen. He is looking down. THE BARTENDER enters.

                    THE BARTENDER
          Hey, Tony. You look white as a
          sheet! Are you okay?

                    TONY
          I've just seen a long time
          girlfriend and her family. It was
          gruesome. She was with their choice
          of a wimp son-in-law.

                    THE BARTENDER
          Hey, Tony, I've known you for all
          the years that I worked at that
          small town hotel, when you lived
          there.

                    TONY
          I remember you well, Scotty.

                    THE BARTENDER
          When you were a little guy in your
          mother's hash joint there, you used
          to take everything seriously. I can
          imagine now. What I didn't tell
          anyone then, was that I left
          Scotland for here, when the same
          thing happened to me.

                    TONY
          That helps to know, I guess.

                    THE BARTENDER
          So, let them go to hell. Just hop
          in your new convertible out there
          and drive off into the sunset. Hey
          guy, enjoy life! See you later. Are
          you okay?

                    TONY
          Yeh, thanks, Scotty.

                                        CUT TO:

INT. OPEN KITCHEN OF SMALL HOME (1967) - NIGHT
CHARACTER #13
TONY'S MOTHER'S HUSBAND, BUZZ. BLOND, RESEMBLES AN OLDER
ROBERT. RED-FACED ALCOHOLIC WITH A CONSISTENT LOATHSOME
SMIRK,

BUZZ is sitting hunched over a kitchen table, with a bottle
of Rye in front of him. TONY enters from the rear outside
door.

                    BUZZ
          So what's this I hear about you
          calling Jake Thomson an ass-hole?
          You're supposed to know better.
          Aren't you the one with all the
          damn education?

                    TONY
          You're telling me how to respond to
          Anne's father? That's hard to
          believe.

                    BUZZ
          Well you should find another
          schoolgirl. Hell, there's lots of
          them around.

                    TONY
          They wouldn't be like Anne. We went
          together a long time. Do you
          understand that we were living
          together? We were planning to get
          married. Why are you thinking that
          she is still a school girl?

                    BUZZ
          Hell, they could all be a piece of
          tail. Hell, lots of them better.

                    TONY
          I was going to marry Anne and we
          were very intimate.

                    BUZZ
               (slurrying his words)
          I can tell you… any of those
          schoolgirls could teach you a thing
          or two about sex. Hey... do you
          think you can still make five
          figures? You're not goin' to be
          nothin'.

TONY leaves the room to pick up his suitcase from the second
bedroom. He takes a look around as if to imply that this is
the last time he'll see inside this house - and leaves. He
pauses at the outside rear door as if to slam it shut, but
instead smiles at his own maturity, pauses, and purposely
shuts it gently.

                                        CUT TO:

INT. MOBILE HOME LIVING ROOM - NIGHT

At a trailer court, with friends, a married couple, TONY has
real estate books and photos that he has shown. He is closing
the books and putting them into his brief case.
CHARACTER #14
CAROL, IS A SMALL, BLOND, FRIENDLY, NICE SMALL TOWN GIRL.
CHARACTER #15
JIM IS SHORT, THE COUNTERPART TO CAROL, THEY ARE A GOOD
MATCH.

                    CAROL
          Now, what about Anne?

                    JIM
          You weren't going to mention that!

TONY looks startled, he pauses before speaking as he
obviously is not able to comprehend the name of ANNE.

TONY
Who? Who's Anne?

CAROL
Anne, you know, your old fiancée,
your old girl friend.

TONY'S expression changes as he is now remembering. He tries
to verbally overcome his former lack of memory.

TONY
Oh, yeh. I don't know. I haven't
seen her for quite awhile.

JIM
We know about you guys at the
lake... you know... after she was
engaged to Robert. Remember? We saw
you there.

TONY
There isn't anything that I can do
about it - unfortunately.

CAROL
(smiling broadly)
Yes there is! She's living here.
I've spoken to her at the shopping
center. Do you want me to contact
her?

JIM
She's crazy, Anne is out of her
tree. Carol and I just don't agree
on this.

CAROL
I think it's romantic. She was
simply doing what her parents
wanted her to do. I want to contact
her if Tony wants me to!

TONY
Okay. I'd really like to get
together with her.

CAROL
Let's do it. I'll talk to her. I'll
phone you in the next few days.

TONY leaves and is shown getting into his new convertible,
looking back at the trailer and nodding to himself as if deep
in thought.

                              DISSOLVE TO:

INT. REAL ESTATE OFFICE - DAY

TONY, well dressed with an expensive suit, is on the phone
from his inner office. It is luxuriously appointed.

                    TONY
          So it's great talking with you
          Anne. I didn't know when you'd
          call. I guess with waiting for
          Robert to be out and your little
          daughter to be asleep, it doesn't
          leave many windows of time.

                    ANNE
          It's great talking to you again,
          Tony. I've really missed you. I
          want to know all about Paris. Tell
          me if it was like you imagined it.

                    TONY
          It was. I only was there for the
          two stays though. I went to Germany
          with a girl friend after a few
          months and then I worked in England
          until I could save enough money to
          return. Paris was where I studied
          though.

                    ANNE
          What about writing? And what about
          painting and music, Tony? What did
          you do? Was it exciting?

                    TONY
          Let's get together and have some
          time to talk all about it. How
          about next week - or sooner?

                    ANNE
          No, I won't get together with you
          Tony. I have a little girl now.

                    TONY
          Trust me. It doesn't matter. That
          would be great. Even bring her
          along. You know that expression: my
          intentions are honourable. They
          still are.

                    ANNE
          I can't have any more children,
          Tony. It wouldn't be fair to you.
          I've wrecked your life enough,
          don't you think?

                    TONY
          I guess that me being just a
          salesman, doesn't help. I guess
          that you know I'm good at it, a
          success.

                    ANNE
          Robert just fixes air-conditioners
          and furnaces for a living. You're
          doing great, Tony. I have to go
          now. Good-by.

                    TONY
          Good-by Anne. Call if you ever
          change your mind. I really would
          still like to marry you.

Music increases in volume such that we only hear Tony's last
words, not showing him hang-up. TONY is shown to be sitting
alone in a very large office space.

                                        DISSOLVE TO:

EXT. HERITAGE HOTEL - NIGHT - ESTABLISHING

INT. LAVISH HERITAGE HOTEL PRESENTATION ROOM INTERIOR - NIGHT

As a well dressed international art dealer, TONY is
presenting the paintings to an established art consumer. He
is wearing a double breasted suit with a turtle necked
sweater. ROBERT is dressed as "country and western casual".

                    TONY
          I purchased the three hundred
          paintings in eleven different
          countries, and hopefully most art
          schools are represented.

ANNE approaches from his side, dressed in a white print dress, wearing no makeup, a fact shown unusual for this era of heavy eye shadow and sprayed hairstyles. They are now twenty six years old.

> ANNE
> Good evening, Tony.

> ROBERT
> (Smirking as he lies,
> oblivious to Tony's
> former contact)
> We drove down from Edmonton. The trip was paid for by our parents, So we had to promise them that we'd drop in to your exhibit.

> TONY
> Glad you could see it. I've only been in real estate two years and I guess this is my academic sideline.

> ROBERT
> So, can you make us a deal?

> TONY
> Sure. I already had thought I would, when I saw you walk in. You can have anything at cost.

> ROBERT
> So what's that?

> TONY
> Just divide by five, or use twenty percent.

ROBERT laughs and looks away from TONY.

> ROBERT
> So you're a rip-off artist!

> TONY
> No. I just have to buy them in another country, speak another language, package them, take them through customs, frame them, present them here - and only then the rest of the profit is mine.

> ROBERT
> Like I said - a rip-off artist.

                    ANNE
          Let's just choose one Robert. We
          want one of Tony's paintings.

                    TONY
          Sure just go ahead. Take your time.
          I'll go and talk to some customers.

TONY meets and is talking to an adult interior design
student, a pretty well dressed redhead, who is a woman (with
children) that he would only pursue for a few months. TONY
glances over to ANNE a number of times with admiration. She
has chosen a painting. He hears her remark to ROBERT.

                    ANNE
          So go ahead, you wanted to have a
          coffee in this hotel. We're here
          now so no one will mind. You can
          just relax. We're buying a painting
          so you don't have to order anything
          costly. That's what you were
          worrying about.

                    ROBERT
          Yeh, okay I'll be in the restaurant
          when you're finished looking at
          this stuff.

                    ANNE
          I just want to stay here a bit and
          watch Tony in his element. This is
          very cool to see.

                                        CUT TO:

INT. COFFEE SHOP IN THE SMALL TOWN HOTEL - DAY

                    ANNE'S MOTHER
          Hi Tony. I asked to be your
          waitress. Maybe you remember me?
          You and my daughter were quite an
          item.

TONY looks blank, then puzzled, then he starts to remember.

                    TONY
          Oh, of course. Yes, I remember you.
          You had me over for dinner years
          ago. Of course.

                    ANNE'S MOTHER
          May I join you? We aren't busy.

                    TONY
          Of course. How are you?

                    ANNE'S MOTHER
          Great, and you? I always wonder
          where you got to.

                    TONY
          I don't know. I guess it's
          important to say that I'm
          successful. I'm now living in
          Calgary in a new four-bedroom home
          that I just built.

                    ANNE'S MOTHER
          That's good, Tony. But, have you
          found someone yet?

                    TONY
          No, but I enjoy my one-third acre
          lot and the view. I like to play
          house with my dates on the
          weekends.

                    ANNE'S MOTHER
          Well Anne and Robert have finally
          overcome their differences and have
          learned to live together
          compatibly.

                    TONY
          Although I knew it was not your
          belief, I still truly believe that
          people shouldn't be married just
          because they are a certain age. I
          truly believe in individuals being
          compatible. I've never, and
          possibly will never find someone as
          perfect for me and me for her, as
          Anne. I'll keep looking, but it
          won't necessarily happen

                    ANNE'S MOTHER
          Let me get your dessert Tony. It's
          my treat.

M.O.S. TONY again thanks her as he leaves, pausing to look
back, still a little puzzled. He later gets in his
convertible, while sitting parked in front of the coffee
shop, just sitting in contemplation. It is the manner of a
man trying to figure it all out.

                                        CUT TO:

INT. A LARGE AIRPLANE (1982)- NIGHT

ANNE, as a flight attendant, approaches TONY as he has now relaxed, as a passenger.

                    ANNE
Do I know you?

                    TONY
      (smiling politely)
I don't think so. Should I?

                    ANNE
We went to school together. We're both from the same town, Tony.

                    TONY
Oh, and I thought it was a pick-up line or something.

                    ANNE
No, we knew each other quite well. What are you doing on this flight? Do you travel to our nation's capital often?

                    TONY
No, there's been a major recession in real estate so I'm working for the federal government as an appraiser and property negotiator. I'm on my way to a course. Sorry, I didn't recognize you right away... We were in grade ten and had a study period together. I remember passing notes to you. We always managed to sit together!

                    ANNE
I'll be able to take a few minutes off. This isn't a full flight so we can talk in one of the seats at the back. I'll arrange it in a minute. I'll be right back.

ANNE returns, with directions for TONY to join her in the back seats of the aircraft. They settle in.

                    TONY
You look exactly like you did in high school.

ANNE
Thanks, Tony. But you don't
remember anything else after that -
- after high school?

TONY
I went to Europe, so not a lot
happened here.

ANNE
Where do you live, Tony?

TONY
On the coast. I just completed
building a new home there. It's
rather unique.

ANNE
Are you married?

TONY
Yes, for over seven years. I
finally settled down.

ANNE
Do you have children?

TONY
Two - a boy and a girl. They're
both preschoolers. Great kids! I'm
very lucky.

ANNE
My mother and her new husband are
moving to the coast. They want to
choose an area. Is it a nice place
to live?

TONY
I love it there. It's as close to
California as Canada ever gets.
Great landscaping everywhere, it's
quite beautiful. We really don't
have much snow - if any.

ANNE
I'll tell them. I really will look
up some statistics. Your weather
sounds wonderful. Thanks, Tony.
I'll be looking forward to visiting
there myself! Maybe we'll even move
there. It was great meeting you
again. I had no idea where you went
to after Calgary.

                    TONY
          I may seem a bit puzzled. Should we
          be having a coffee or something
          after the flight?

                    ANNE
          No, but just leave it to me. We'll
          definitely meet again.

                                        DISSOLVE TO:

INT. RECREATIONAL ROOM, EARLY CANADIAN STYLE (1984) -
ESTABLISHING

TONY is looking at the High School yearbook. One third of the
page sports a photo of TONY and ANNE kissing. He has a tight
perm Afro hairstyle in 1984, with a different specific style
shown in the 1961 photo.

INSERT WITH AN EXTREME CLOSE UP OF THE PHOTO. IT IS FRAMED AS
A HEART.

TONY walks out doors with the yearbook and puts it into the
garbage can. He looks down the road and shakes his head
slowly, showing a thought pattern.

                                        CUT TO:

INT. FOYER OF LARGE NEWER HOME - DAY

TONY is having an open house on one of his listings for sale.
It is an exclusive and expensive house. ROBERT and ANNE walk
in. TONY does not recognize them.

                    ROBERT
          Hi, we're a new family to the area.
          Do you mind if we make an
          inspection?

                    TONY
          Sure, come right through. That's
          why we have the opens.

ROBERT begins to head off by himself, with ANNE hesitating.

                    TONY (CONT'D)
          I'll give you the tour though. It's
          a very nice home. You'll especially
          like the view.
                    (MORE)

                    TONY (CONT'D)
Just to the left here we have an
incredible guest suite. You've gone
this direction, so lets start here.

                    ROBERT
We just want to see the house. We
don't want your company.

                    TONY
Unfortunately, the sellers still
live here. I do have to accompany
everyone as they go through.

                    ROBERT
Well not us. Don't you trust us?

                    TONY
Sorry. It's a five thousand square
foot home - presently lived in with
personal belongings. I do need to
accompany you.

                    ROBERT
Who do you work for? We live in
this subdivision now. Do you have
training in showing exclusive
homes?

                    TONY
More than you can imagine.

                    ROBERT
I need to talk to your sales
manager.

                    TONY
I guess that you have a problem in
complaining. I'm the managing
broker of my company.

                    ROBERT
Have you ever lived in a house like
this? When salespeople come in from
outside of the area, they're not
familiar with the sophistication
needed in these higher priced
homes.

                    TONY
My family and I live just five
homes down. Actually my home is
slightly larger.

                    ROBERT
          Well, you don't tell me that we
          can't go through because you don't
          trust us. I'll report you to
          someone.

                    ANNE
          We can just go through, Robert. It
          would be great to hear a
          presentation of a home like this.

ROBERT heads into the foyer and out the door. ANNE hesitates
in the foyer.

                    ROBERT
          No. We can also just go. We're
          leaving.

                    ANNE
          This is terrible. I'm sorry. He
          didn't notice your name on the
          sign. This just isn't fair.

TONY shows his usual easygoing self, obviously not
understanding who the individuals were, consistently smiling
as in a normal sales presentation.

                    TONY
          It's alright, it's okay - I'm used
          to it - I sell for a living.

                    ANNE
          It's not fair, especially not with
          you.

                                        DISSOLVE TO:

EXT. OPEN HOUSE SIGN OF SAME LARGER NEWER HOME - DAY -
ESTABLISHING

INT. LIVING ROOM OF SAME LARGER NEWER HOME - CONTINUOUS

                    ANNE
          I waited until no one else was
          around, Tony. I came by to talk to
          you. Could we speak candidly?

                    TONY
          Sure... Why not?

                    ANNE
You don't seem to remember me. Do
you remember anything? Do you
remember us being engaged?

                    TONY
I only remember high school. We
passed notes back and forth in
grade ten.

                    ANNE
There was a lot more than that - -
for years after that.

                    TONY
I just don't remember.

                    ANNE
My marriage doesn't exist anymore.
It never existed actually. If your
marriage is on the rocks, we should
work at figuring this all out. We
should be together, Tony.

                    TONY
My marriage is lousy, but like all
marriages, we have to work at it. I
have two young children, so I'm
definitely obligated

                    ANNE
Do you remember anything about us
going together?

                    TONY
We should have gone together. I
remember you passing one specific
note that asked whether I believed
in oral sex. I wrote back, "Not
with animals". You had burst out
laughing, breaking the quietness of
the study hall. I'll never forget
the fun of that particular joke.

                    ANNE
I'll go now, but I'll be around,
Tony. I'm not going anywhere. We
rent just down the hill from you -
we're in this subdivision because
we're house sitting... See you
later, Tony.

                                    CUT TO:

EXT. AT AN OPEN AREA PARK - NIGHT
CHARACTER #16
SUSAN, TONY'S DAUGHTER IS INITIALLY A VERY CUTE FOUR-YEAR OLD
BRUNETTE.
CHARACTER #17
PAUL, TONY'S SON, BLOND. INITIALLY HE IS SIX MONTHS OLD.

A fireworks display is being set up for the residence of the
subdivision. ANNE and ROBERT are already there as ROBERT is
helping with the set-up. TONY, his wife BETTY and his two
children join the group. BETTY finds another woman to visit
with. Tony's one-year-old son PAUL is in a pack on his chest,
and SUSAN is at his side.

                    ANNE
          I know that you don't remember me,
          but I would really like to stand
          here with you and your children -
          as being someone you had attended
          high school with.

                    TONY
          Sure, that sounds completely
          logical.

                    ANNE
          It's great that you found a pack
          for Paul that works on your chest.
          It's superior to the one that I
          used. It only carried my daughter
          on my back and I couldn't watch
          her.

ANNE looks down and around at SUSAN and laughs.

                    ANNE (CONT'D)
          She's holding on to her Daddy's
          finger for dear life!

                    SUSAN
          My Daddy and I like the red and
          blue fireworks best. Sometimes we
          like green, but not much.

                    ROBERT
               (looks back and joins
                them)
          Hey guy, couldn't you have helped?

                    TONY
          Unfortunately I'm with my children.
          Kids first, then the fireworks.

                    ANNE
                (turning to Robert)
        You said that the main safety worry
        was that too many people would want
        to be involved.

                    ROBERT
        Well did you at least pay the ten
        dollars that each resident was
        supposed to pay?

                    TONY
        I definitely did that. I can still
        help if you want.

ROBERT leaves and goes back to the small cluster of men
standing to the side. TONY purposely stands beside ANNE, with
his children, for the duration of the fireworks, although he
doesn't know why.

                                        CUT TO:

INT. FOYER OF LARGE WEST COAST CONTEMPORARY HOME - NIGHT
CHARACTER #18
LESE, ANNE'S DAUGHTER, PRETTY, SEVENTEEN, IN STYLE (1985)

LESE is going out the door, speaking to TONY as he stands
beside her, holding the door and looking out.

                    LESE
        The kids were great and they went
        to sleep right on time! Good night
        to you both. My mother is waiting
        outside. I had just phoned her to
        pick me up.

TONY opens the door and stands transfixed, frozen by seeing
the vehicle outside, where ANNE is sitting in the driver's
seat.

                    TONY
        Say hello to your mother in the
        car.

                                    DISSOLVE TO:

EXT. BACK YARD WITH SIDE ACCESS - DAY

TONY is weeding his rose garden. ANNE is standing beside him.
They are at the side of the house.

> ANNE
> I always look down here when I'm
> jogging by - - just in case I can
> say hello to you when you're
> working outside.

> TONY
> Thanks. I enjoy the break from
> constant house and yard work. Large
> homes aren't necessary fun. It's
> like maintaining a resort.

> ANNE
> Those are beautiful roses. I also
> noticed a fruit tree. What kind is
> it?

> TONY
> It's a peach tree. It's
> interesting. It won't bear fruit
> unless I plant another peach tree
> nearby.

> ANNE
> You might think about that process
> and maybe apply it to me... Does
> Betty appreciate the fact that you
> grow such wonderful roses for her?
> It's absolutely great the way some
> of them bloom alternatively three
> seasons of the year.

> TONY
> No, she complains that I never buy
> her flowers from a commercial
> florist. She's enthralled with
> spending money.

> ANNE
> (speaking almost in a
> whisper)
> If I stand here silently, could you
> actually see me?

DISSOLVE TO:

EXT. ROOF TOP WITH FRONT SIDEWALK NEAR - DAY

TONY is on his roof cleaning the large skylights. ANNE is jogging by and she stops.

> ANNE
> I thought that you used to be
> afraid of heights.

> TONY
> When I built this house, I got over
> it... I had no choice.

> ANNE
> I wish you could see our small town
> from there.

TONY is looking down smiling. He says nothing more and ANNE carries on jogging.

CUT TO:

EXT. BACK YARD BLOCK PARTY (1986) WITH A HOT TUB - NIGHT

> NEIGHBOR #1
> So, Tony. Let's get this straight.
> You were building the Lutheran
> Church and needed to get rid of a
> lot of soil from the excavation. To
> save money, you had it all hauled
> to the vacant lots here in the
> subdivision and the lots became a
> park?

> TONY
> The city already had bought the
> fourteen lots and declared them
> park. It's just that the lots were
> swamp before.

> NEIGHBOR #1
> So now they'll maintain it as a
> park?

> TONY
> Right. I also had one of our
> bulldozers stop off here and level
> it. The city is seeding the grass.
> So it was very little cost to the
> city.

                         NEIGHBOR #1
               It just happens to be three lots
               away from your house.

                         TONY
                    (smiling widely)
               Everybody wins!

TONY walks over, with his drink, to where a number of
neighbors are in a hot tub. He notices ANNE is near the tub,
in a full piece bathing suit.

                         NEIGHBOR #2
               Hey Tony! You could say that this
               is the party celebrating our new
               park. We're glad that you could
               come.

                         TONY
               I wouldn't miss it. It's not like I
               had a long walk! I live across the
               street.

TONY notices that ROBERT is pacing around the pool, quite out
of place, as he is fully dressed almost formally.

                         NEIGHBOR #3
               If you don't mind me asking... Two
               churches were built this year.
               Yours and the larger Baptist
               church. You were the project
               manager or general contractor of
               one, so you're obviously involved
               in the church. So my question is:
               Why two? What's the need?

                         TONY
               There is a fundamental difference
               in the way we do things. It has to
               do with the question of: Why don't
               fundamentalists have sex standing
               up? The theological reason is that
               it is because it might lead to
               dancing.
AD LIB within the group and laughter

                         NEIGHBOR #2
                    (still laughing)
               I'm guessing that did actually
               explain the differences. I grew up
               with some fundamentalists.

TONY begins to move towards the house. Seeing this, ANNE gets
up and moves the same direction to the house and into the
kitchen area. She then stands with her back against the
cabinets. TONY enters the kitchen last.

> ANNE
> Tony, do you remember me in a dark
> blue swimming suit? I had worn it a
> lot at Gull Lake.

> TONY
> No, but I obviously should have.

ROBERT barges in, as if in an emergency.

> ROBERT
> Can I have my wife back now?

TONY motions to the WIFE AND OWNER, Anne's friend, who is now
standing to the side of the room.

> TONY
> Oh is this your wife, sorry, I was
> only visiting.

> ROBERT
> You see Anne! You don't wear a
> swimming suit to a party! They just
> told me out there, about the
> insults. I told you that you needed
> to dress properly!

> ANNE
> (laughing)
> You definitely wear a swimming suit
> to a hot tub party!

The MALE HOME OWNER enters the kitchen, from having been
taking a shower. He is intoxicated.

> MALE HOME OWNER
> Hi Robert. What seems to be the
> problem?

> ROBERT
> This rabble insulted my wife with a
> joke about our religion!

> ANNE
> It wasn't that bad - - it was very
> funny.

                    MALE HOME OWNER
          Well Tony, you'll just have to
          leave. I'm not going to allow this.

                    THE WIFE AND OWNER (O.C.)
          You must be joking. That's
          ridiculous. We're having a party to
          celebrate the park across the
          street and you're asking Tony to
          leave? He built it!

                    MALE HOME OWNER
          I back up Robert through thick and
          thin. Whatever he says goes,
          especially about religion.

                    THE WIFE AND OWNER (O.C.)
          We might also have a say in this.
          Anne and I were trying to
          accomplish something here.

                    MALE HOME OWNER
          Robert says his wife has been
          insulted and that's the end of it.

TONY turns to leave and proceeds to the doorway.

                    TONY
          No problem! See you guys later!

The neighbors have noticed a confrontation of sorts and they
move to stand in the open sliding glass doors to the pool
area.

                    NEIGHBOR #2
          What's happening guys?

                    TONY
               (smiling)
          I've just been asked to leave
          because my jokes were too bad. I'll
          have to work on them!

AD LIB: The neighbors shake their heads in disbelief.

                    ROBERT
          Some people never learn how to
          behave!

ROBERT then turns to TONY, who is still standing at the door.

>   ROBERT (CONT'D)
>   And you take credit for building a
>   church while you're not even a Born
>   Again Christian. You cannot be on
>   the road to Christ lest ye be born
>   again.
>
>   TONY
>   Wow.

TONY shakes his head and then waves nonchalantly as he exits
out the front door.

AD LIB: The background chatter (to the music) is about
religion, with the two owners of the home arguing about the
stupidity of asking TONY to leave. ANNE is arguing with
ROBERT.

>   CUT TO:

EXT. ON SIDEWALK IN FRONT OF CHURCH - NIGHT

A 1987 new Buick had pulled over to the curb in front of the
recently built contemporary styled church. A "live nativity
scene" made up of TONY and six other members of his church
has been set up next to the main entrance of the Lutheran
church. THE MEMBERS are dressed in costume. SUSAN now
thirteen is acting as the Virgin Mary. Anne's father, JAKE,
now with white hair, gets out of the driver's seat and
approaches TONY. ROBERT moves up to the driver's seat.

>   JAKE
>   You may not remember me, but I will
>   never forget you. You worked for me
>   for a couple of years unloading
>   drilling mud at my warehouse. You
>   were in high school. I'm Jake
>   Thomson.
>
>   TONY
>   No, sorry, I don't remember you. As
>   far as drilling mud goes, I worked
>   for Bruce Magilton. But, I did know
>   some Thomson's from Tees.
>
>   JAKE
>   Bruce was my man in charge. Well,
>   the Thomson's from Tees are here
>   too. My brother Sid, a man you got
>   along with well, has passed away.
>   His widow Ida, is here in the front
>   seat.

TONY acknowledges the lady in the front seat, by approaching
the car, turning towards her.

> TONY
> I'm pleased to see you again Ida.
> We last met at Buzz Lawson's
> funeral in Tees. You were in the
> lady's group that was hired to
> provide sandwiches. I'm sorry to
> hear about Sid.

> LADY IN CAR
> Yes, he always said good things
> about you. He would be pleased that
> you remembered.

> TONY
> Sid used to take me duck hunting
> when I was about eight years old.
> We lived for short periods in Tees.
> His hunting trips were important to
> me. You had lived across the street
> from Babe and Bernard, the two
> uncles of Buzz. Babe was the
> pedophile and Bernard could declare
> with pride, that he had literally
> never worked. You knew us all well.

ROBERT yells from the driver's seat of his father-in-law's
new Buick, where he is now sitting proudly.

> ROBERT
> And you admit that?

> TONY
> I was a kid, just visiting at the
> time. I've always stated it that
> way - I was just visiting that
> environment.

> JAKE
> Well, I can tell you that your
> father would be very proud of you
> for having built this great
> structure. I understand you were
> completely in charge as project
> manager. That is really something,
> for us from your past to see. You
> know, I used to ice fish with your
> father, Buzz.

                    TONY
          Actually, my father was Emile, from
          Dawson Creek. But Buzz married my
          mother. To tell it like it was,
          Buzz would never adopt me, which in
          hindsight is great - I don't have
          to think of myself as being from
          his family. As you knew them, I'm
          sure I don't have to explain
          myself. I'm sure you understand
          completely.

                    JAKE
          I guess I never had all the facts.
          You know you were always your own
          man and then some. What did your
          real father do for a living?

                    TONY
          He was a carpenter and a
          construction project manager. Yes,
          if he had seen this church, I'm
          sure he would have been proud of
          me.

                    JAKE
          I'm very sure he would have been
          proud throughout your entire life.
          Has your family ever been involved
          in the church, or in church work?

TONY is bemused, but not knowing why, he smiles politely.

                    TONY
          Actually, I've learned that once
          every four generations, one of us
          has been a project manager for
          building a church. I didn't know
          that when I began this project, but
          one of my aunts reminded me. Over
          the last twelve generations, my
          family has volunteered as the
          builder, on at least three
          churches. That's not a lot, but
          it's consistent.

                    LADY IN CAR
               (begins to laugh)
          I can see you do it quite
          naturally... You know I would have
          made the trip out here just to hear
          you say that.
                    (MORE)

                    LADY IN CAR (CONT'D)
My Sid never liked the church, but
he sure would have got a kick out
of this and what you've done.

                    TONY
Thanks.

                    JAKE
Don't you think of yourself as
being from our neck of the woods
anymore? You knew a lot of people
there and a lot of people knew you.
I've met many of them who have
asked after you, and many who have
wished you well.

                    TONY
Honestly, I really only knew my
fellow high school students.

                    JAKE
I really do know a lot of older
folks who remember you well.

                    TONY
I've thought about it a lot and
I've come to the conclusion that
because the Lawson family didn't
chum around with the normal groups
of people, I really don't know many
of the families there. I don't
remember many last names. Often
I've been asked if I know someone
back there, and I usually don't, so
I just mention that I'm originally
from Dawson Creek. It's just easier
to explain.

                    ANNE
It makes sense for you to just
think that you were from Dawson
Creek, Tony.

                    LESE
          (waving from the back
          seat)
Hi, do you remember me? I used to
baby sit your kids!

                    TONY
Oh. Hi Lese. Of course. How's
university?

          LESE
Great. Interesting, just like you
said it would be.

TONY bends down to look into the back seat to talk to LESE.

          TONY
Did you take the subjects that you
wanted to take? Even biology and
science?

          LESE
Yes, In spite of it all - - I took
the ones that I wanted.

          TONY
That's Great!

          LESE
My mother told me that your life is
a real rags to riches story. Just
as your house is one of the largest
in Delta, you grew up in really bad
shacks. We drove by it - - just to
show Granddad your beautiful
Christmas lights and its design.

          TONY
I'm sure that you understand what I
mean when I say materialism and a
high standard of living are not my
greatest achievement. My
accomplishment is being a church
builder and in achieving "Life in
Christ", not only for myself, but
for my family.

          JAKE
That's really summing it all up!

          ROBERT
But to be a real church builder you
have to be born again. You people
here are just heathens.

          TONY
Oh, I think by some definitions we
are born again by our evolution of
new thoughts and outlooks.

                    JAKE
          I have something to say about that,
          Robert. We can at least be
          respectful of an old friend, a very
          good friend. I'd like to talk to
          Tony, Robert.

JAKE steps two steps away from the car, now being closer to
TONY, who also has stepped back.

                    JAKE (CONT'D)
          Tony, if you don't mind, I would
          like to ask you a couple of
          questions about our past. I'm sure
          I knew you well back then. Do you
          remember some church people,
          perhaps part of my group?

                    TONY
          The college on the edge of town was
          Seventh Day Adventist. I had some
          friends my age from that community.

                    JAKE
          What about some of the evangelical
          and fundamentalist families? Do you
          remember them?

                    TONY
          Sorry, that I don't remember. The
          area was predominately Dutch. They
          may have been Dutch Reform or
          Calvinists. There are a lot of
          names that I've forgotten from that
          area. I really only used the first
          names of so many of my classmates,
          so I've forgotten their last names.

                    JAKE
          You didn't know it at the time, but
          you may have been my best friend.
          We were involved in a group that I
          am told by most definitions was a
          cult. How about before that time?
          Do you remember what you did for
          the Koch family? I guess you would
          only be about seven years old.

                    ANNE
          Six years old.

                    JAKE
You were the only one brave enough
to report the ongoing sexual abuse
of their daughter. Even though
you'd been threatened, you were the
only one in the entire school who
would come forward. Her family
never forgot you.

                    TONY
I remember it completely.

                    JAKE
Well, in many later years, I've
been accused of spearheading,
conniving and even leading a group
against you. I don't guess I was -
I know that I was - and those
accusations are true. I've always
been sorry for my actions. I would
give anything to be able to turn
back the clock and do things
differently this time.

                    ROBERT
He's not a Christian. He's not
been born again.

                    TONY
        (ignoring Robert, speaking
         directly to Jake)
I don't think whatever you did
could have been that bad.

                    JAKE
Well, if you ever remember it, I
would definitely like to discuss
it. What do you remember about the
adults against the teenagers in the
fifties and sixties?

                    TONY
Often in my public speaking in the
church, I have been asked about my
impression of the fifties. I
usually say that it was not a time
when teenagers began to rebel as is
often stated. It was a time when
the adult world was very uptight.
They were so uptight that they
worried about which side we parted
our hair in a literal sense. The
color of our clothes even seemed
important.

JAKE
We were worse than that. I was one
of those adults and I not only had
blinders on, I couldn't see two
feet in front of me. I hope that
some day you will understand and
forgive me.

TONY
I'm sure it's not a problem.

JAKE
Does your daughter over there
understand your religion?

TONY
She's excited this Christmas. In
mid-January I'll be in Israel for
three weeks. The trip is through
the travel agency that I own. So
this year when she hears about the
star of Bethlehem, she knows that
next month I'll be there. It seems
to make the Holy Land very real to
both her and my son.

LADY IN CAR
I've heard you've travelled a lot.
How many countries have you
visited, Tony?

TONY
Forty-three with the Middle East
now. I've been very fortunate. This
visit to Israel is such that I may
put together a system for church
tour groups.

ROBERT
It's pouring rain, Dad. Get in the
car before you get sick.

JAKE
No. No, this is a very rare time
when I get to talk about some
happenings of a long time ago. When
Tony worked for me he was one of my
best workers even though he was
only in high school. In fact he was
the best worker I've ever had. It's
no surprise that he built this
church here along with the big
house up on the hill. I should have
known he'd do something great.

                    ROBERT
Well, talk to your old cronies when
it's not pouring rain. This is
ridiculous.

                    ANNE
It's not raining that hard. Tony,
it's great to hear you talking
about our past.

                    LESE
Yeah, get in Grandpa, you'll get
wet.

                    ROBERT
This religion and this church are
all wet! Let's go! Dad, get in and
sit down.

                    JAKE
Listen young man, when I'm talking
to someone. And especially when it
is as important as this... I don't
want to be interrupted and told
where and when to sit.

                    ROBERT
Loony Tunes, that's what it is!
This guy's a phoney - he's a con
man!

                    JAKE
Well, it seems the pressure is on.
All right, I'll get in the car.
Here, I'll just roll down the
window. Are you okay out there,
Tony? I presume that hood on your
wise man costume keeps you dry.

                    TONY
Sure, I'm okay... I should tell you
though, we usually have some sheep
in our nativity scene. But this
year we had a problem getting any.

                    ANNE
What was the problem, Tony?

                    TONY
The Lutheran farmer that we usually
get some from moved. We had a
chance to borrow another farmer's
sheep, but then we found out that
the family was fundamentalist.
                    (MORE)

> TONY (CONT'D)
> So, they were fundamentalist sheep.
> We looked around, but just couldn't
> find any Lutheran sheep.

Laughter follows, with LESE laughing the loudest.

> ROBERT
> That's blasphemy!

> LADY IN CAR
> I've heard about your humour, Tony.
> This has been the highlight of my
> trip to the coast.

ANNE briefly opens her back passenger car door, on the
opposite side. She stands up to talk over the car to TONY.

> ANNE
> Good-bye, Tony. I'll definitely
> check out a service or two in your
> new church.

> ROBERT
> I won't allow any such thing!

> LESE
> So long!

The car now drives slowly away, passing the "living nativity
scene" and the other church members in their costumes. ROBERT
is heard shouting out of his driver's side window.

> ROBERT
> Heathens, lest ye shall be born
> again! Loony Tunes!

> DISSOLVE TO:

INT. CHURCH WASHROOM - MOMENTS LATER

TONY is throwing cold water on his face from the washroom
sink in the church. He is still wearing his wise man costume
and he observes his shaking hands. The MINISTER, who has been
a part of the nativity scene, joins him in the washroom.

> MINISTER
> That young fellow seemed really
> uptight. I've never seen a
> fundamentalist that was that
> uptight, especially over something
> like a nativity scene.

                    TONY
          It's okay. They're just from a
          small town in Alberta.

                    MINISTER
          I had given them a tour of the new
          building. They were really
          impressed. They seemed to indicate
          that they'd known you well, even
          since childhood.

                    TONY
          They're one of the many families
          that I've run across from where I
          attended high school. The woman in
          the front has known me since
          elementary school

                    MINISTER
          Are you okay? Your face is sheer
          white.

                    TONY
          I'm okay. I guess this garb is too
          hot.

                                        CUT TO:

INT. COMMUNITY SKATING RINK (1992) - NIGHT

TONY is skating with his son, PAUL, who is now eleven, and
who is skating separately with his friends.

TONY looks up and sees ANNE and LESE with wide smiles,
watching him through the front glass area. He skates to the
waiting room door to join them. At some mental level he
recognizes them. PAUL simultaneously skates up to TONY, and
they enter the waiting room.

                    PAUL
          Hi, Dad. We can go now if you want.

                    TONY
          Okay, Paul. I want to talk to
          someone I just noticed in the
          waiting room.

                    PAUL
          Sure, but could you help me with my
          skates first. I have a knot that I
          can't get undone.

TONY and PAUL sit on a bench taking Paul's skates off and
ANNE walks over and stands beside them.

>   ANNE
>   Hi, Tony. I don't remember you
>   being able to skate. You know you
>   didn't when you were younger.

>   TONY
>   It's one of those things I learned
>   to do as a father, I guess... This
>   is part of my life style... as
>   someone newly single.

>   ANNE
>   What do you mean, you're not
>   married?

>   TONY
>   No. I'm separated. I've been
>   legally separated for a few months
>   now.

>   ANNE
>   Let me gather my thoughts. Are you
>   okay? Is everything else okay? I
>   can tell you that I definitely know
>   what I want to do.

>   TONY
>   Oh, sure. I'm just letting anyone
>   who wants to know, about my ever
>   changing life styles.

>   ANNE
>   I just have to go out to the car
>   with my daughter. I'll talk to you
>   again... in a minute... Okay?

TONY finishes taking off his own skates. He and PAUL move
over to the opposite end of the room, where they have left
their coats. ANNE and LESE, as well as ROBERT, are making an
exit. LESE and ROBERT go out the door and ANNE walks quickly
over to TONY and PAUL.

>   ANNE (CONT'D)
>   How are you doing Paul? I don't
>   know if you remember me, but my
>   daughter was your baby-sitter. Do
>   you remember Lese?

>   PAUL
>   Sort of.

                    ANNE
I saw you skating and almost didn't
recognize you, as you've grown up
so much, Paul. How are you and your
Dad doing? Are you involved with
lots of things together?

                    PAUL
Sure! We're in Sea Scouts and we
really do lots of things there. We
sail and camp on weekends... We
also play guitar together.

                    ANNE
I told my husband that I just
wanted to come back and say hello
because of the changes in your
life. I'm really happy to see you
both again, Tony.

                    TONY
I live only a few blocks away from
the kids... I can shuttle my
children around, just like living
under one roof. It was a very
civilized separation. Not a lot has
changed. Only dating.

                    ANNE
I know what I want to do. I'll look
for a good divorce lawyer.

                    TONY
Great to see you Anne. Are you
around town at all? We could meet
for a coffee anytime.

                    ANNE
No, unfortunately I'm not around.
We're just visiting today. But be
assured that I'll definitely be in
touch.

                    LESE
          (re-entering the skating
          rink)
Mom, hurry up. Dad is waiting in
the car and he's just fuming. You
know how he is when he gets mad.
          (looking at Tony)
He's out there pouting as usual.

                    ANNE
          Well, he'll have to get used to it.
          As of today a lot of things have
          changed that he has to get used to.

                    TONY
          Are we causing confusion?

                    ANNE
          No, it's just us. There's always
          confusion. I'll be in touch, Tony.
          I'm going to be busy for awhile,
          and then we'll run into each other
          again... Bye, Paul, have fun in Sea
          Scouts and everything!

                                        DISSOLVE TO:

INT. SHOPPING MALL (1997) - DAY

                    ANNE
          Hi, Tony! I was just with Susan for
          an aesthetics appointment. My nails
          look great! How are you? Susan just
          told me that you are engaged... and
          to a Pentecostal preacher's former
          wife. That's interesting.

                    TONY
          It's about that time. I've been
          single this time for about four
          years. I guess that you are one of
          Susan's first clients.

ANNE looks in the window of the Hallmark Card shop next door
and TONY joins her.

                    ANNE
          Do you think that any of those
          cards might help me out of the mess
          my life is in?

                    TONY
          Is your life in a mess?

                    ANNE
          Yes, I haven't gotten back to you
          for a reason. I would give anything
          if one of those cards could come
          from the past.
                    (MORE)

ANNE (CONT'D)
Do you have anything from your past
that you wish you could set aside
or that you would do differently?
That you can remember?

TONY
No, my past has been perfectly
taken care of.

ANNE
Even from years ago? Don't you have
any traumatic memories that you
wish you didn't have? Do you have
any memory flashbacks... At all?

TONY
No, not at all. But good luck in
putting your own life together.

ANNE
Good luck to you also, Tony. I'm
definitely going to get my life
back together - finally... Bye for
now.

ANNE walks away with her head down, with TONY observing her.

CUT TO:

EXT. WALKING AND BIKE PATH ON A DYKE - DAY
CHARACTER #19
LESLIE, TONY'S SECOND WIFE. A BLOND BOMBER, ALTHOUGH ALWAYS
DRESSED WITH SOPHISTICATION.

LESLIE and TONY are riding mountain bikes on an ocean dyke (a
stretch of mound about six feet high). Out of boredom, TONY
rides into the ditch and out again. As he rides downward, he
sees ANNE and HER LADY FRIEND approaching. TONY immediately
turns upward, hits loose gravel and wipes out. He is sprawled
on the ground. ANNE immediately runs to Tony's side, and is
beside him as he sits up. LESLIE remains posing, standing
beside her bike at the dyke top.

ANNE
Are you alright?

TONY
I only hurt my pride.

                         ANNE
          Oh, I'm sure you're more than a
          little secure, so that will heal
          quickly... Seriously though, let's
          see your hand. It's bleeding.

ANNE tenderly holds his hand as she takes it in hers.

                         TONY
          Thanks for assisting.

                         ANNE
          It's scraped badly... But, I'm sure
          that as a Scout leader you have
          bandages with you?

                         TONY
          Actually, I do have a first aid kit
          right here in my bike saddlebag.
          I'll use the bandages. Thank you
          very much!

ANNE lets go of his hand and stands back with a sensuous
smile, focusing only on TONY.

                         ANNE
          I knew you'd be prepared. I knew
          you'd still have the Scout in you.
          So stay prepared, but so long for
          now - just for now!

TONY watches her join her LADY FRIEND, being completely
mesmerized. He wipes the gravel from his wounded hand and
continues watching.

                                        CUT TO:

EXT. WALKING AND BIKE PATH ON A DYKE - DAY - MOMENTS LATER

                         LESLIE
          Have you forgotten the lady back
          there yet?

TONY answers, looking away from his wife, not understanding
why he was so drawn to this stranger.

                         TONY
          Of course. I'm sure she was just a
          nurse or something.

                                        CUT TO:

INT. SMALL APARTMENT LIVING ROOM - NIGHT (2003)
CHARACTER #20
LORI IS A FRIEND OF TONY FROM ONE PRIOR DATE. SHE IS BLOND,
FAIRLY GOOD LOOKING AND IS A RED-NECK. SHE DRESSES REASONABLY
WELL. SHE IS A CONTROLLER OF OTHERS BY NATURE.
CHARACTER #21
LUCIENNE IS THE OWNER OF THE SUITE, ANNE'S BEST FRIEND. SHE
PRESENTS HERSELF AS A NICE PERSON AND SHE IS A FLIGHT
ATTENDANT THAT HAS WORKED WITH ANNE FOR OVER TEN YEARS.

LORI receives TONY at an apartment party. She answers the
door as he knocks and throws her arms around him to kiss him.
A surprised TONY finds this amusing, as he had not bothered
to ask for a second date, after their initial date for
drinks. She has phoned him and has invited him to this party.
LUCIENNE stands beside LORI as TONY enters, for some reason
observing the details of the kiss.

                    LUCIENNE
          Hi, I'm Lucienne and I live here.
          That was some kiss. You must be
          Tony.

                    TONY
          Hi. It was a surprise. Am I one of
          the first here?

                    LORI
          Someone has to be first. John is
          already here. Come on in, you can
          visit with John in the living room.
          We'll get some snacks ready.

AD LIB conversation exists between TONY and JOHN, when others
begin to arrive. When ANNE walks into the center of the
party, TONY is talking to a very nice looking thirty-
something blond by the name of DANIELLE. He overhears Anne's
comments, but does not recognize her.

                    LUCIENNE
          Hi, Anne. You decided to come to
          the party after all.

                    ANNE
          I wouldn't miss it for the world!

TONY purposely leaves his discussion and proceeds into the
next room, in order to approach ANNE and LUCIENNE, who seemed
to be in some sort of friendly discussion.

                    LUCIENNE
          So, Tony. Come and sit down and
          tell us about yourself.

                    TONY
               (smiling and relaxed)
          Thanks. I'm pretty straight forward
          with not a lot to tell.

                    LUCIENNE
          I was just told that you're newly
          separated or divorced - or maybe
          newly committed. Which is true?

                    TONY
          To be candid, I'm very single, but
          twice divorced. I guess that makes
          me a two-time looser.

                    ANNE
               (laughing)
          Well maybe it means third-time
          lucky!

                    TONY
               (more serious than
                necessary)
          I guess I believe that
          relationships aren't a circumstance
          of luck... Maybe they're even a
          thing that requires training.

TONY notices how sad ANNE looks. He shows a feeling of having
to retreat. He smiles politely and moves back into the
kitchen for a new discussion with DANIELLE. He quickly gets
Danielle's phone number for a future coffee date.
CHARACTER #22
DR. BILL, A PSYCHIATRIST, IS IN HIS LATE FIFTIES, HE IS ONE
OF MANY MEDICAL PEOPLE PRESENT, HOWEVER, NONE ARE IDENTIFIED
AS SUCH. HE IS THE ONLY ONE WEARING A WHITE SHIRT AND TIE.

The party is into its second hour and is now a noisier
gathering. The living room area and kitchen are joined and
everyone is within a large circle.

                    BILL
          Tony, I hear that you've been
          involved with church music as a
          soloist and I know that it may be
          unusual, but how about singing one
          of your songs? I know that you're
          used to singing in public.

                    TONY
          Fine, if you really want it.

TONY sings a slow song called JESUS. As he sings the portion where he can really give it a blues style, he looks over at ANNE and smiles, as if to share his newly improved style with an old friend. ANNE smiles back, as if enjoying something from the past. There is clapping and accolades at the completion. Optional one minute of singing.

>   LORI
> If that's what church music sounds
> like, I may even go to church!

>   LUCIENNE
> How about something else like that?
> That really was Elvis like.

AD LIB conversation, along with song requests. TONY does a number of Elvis Presley ballads. All of them had been sung to ANNE. Upon occasion TONY would pause and look at ANNE with a puzzled look. As he sang the words of "I GOT A WOMAN, WAY ACROSS TOWN, SHE'S GOOD TO ME" - he looked at ANNE with a look of complete bewilderment. Optional one minute of singing. TONY then speaks directly to ANNE.

>   TONY
> What's your favorite style of
> music? Do you have a preference?

>   ANNE
> I was brought up on Western music.

>   TONY
> Me too. I've always loved to hate
> it.

TONY sings "POOR BOY", a song that he knew he had nailed the Elvis style in. He looked at ANNE again, as if to share a joke for the past. Optional one minute of singing.

>   WOMAN #1
> Would you sing, "DON'T"? I loved
> that song.

As TONY finished the song he pauses and raises his arms in a mock conductor style and all the women sang the last word, "DON'T", with him. When he sings some of the early Elvis; such as "I WANT YOU, I NEED YOU, I LOVE YOU" and lines like, "TREAT ME MEAN AND CRUEL, BUT LOVE ME", he looks at ANNE. Optional one minute of singing.

>   TONY
> A lot of those songs were about
> being in codependency or being
> dysfunctional.

                    ANNE
          A lot of us have learned about
          relationships since.

TONY happily delivers his imitations of Dean Martin, Frankie
Lane, Paul Anka, and others. When he completes the song, "YOU
ARE MY DESTINY", TONY looks at ANNE and shrugs. It seems that
he almost knows her. Optional one minute of singing.

                    BILL
          Tony, what was the highest note
          ever sung in an Elvis Presley
          movie?

                    TONY
          It would have been the opening
          scene in King Creole. Elvis goes to
          the window and looks down the
          street that is obviously New
          Orleans. An elderly lobster and
          crawfish sales lady was pushing her
          cart slowly in front of this
          window. Then you hear the highest
          note sung in an Elvis movie:
               (as a high pitch soprano)
          "CRAWFISH, CRAW AW AW AWFISH".

AD LIB with much laughter.

                    WOMAN #2
          I think I've been had.

TONY sings "YOUNG DREAMS", from the same movie. He sings it
directly to ANNE and ended with the words "EVERY MORNING,
NOON AND NIGHT". Optional one minute of singing.

                    ANNE
          We did it that often, if only you
          remembered.

                    TONY
          I'm sorry, I don't.

                    BILL
          Was there one song that you sang
          more often than any other - when
          you were in your youth? Say when
          you were driving down the highway?

TONY sings, "I'VE BEEN TRAVELLING OVER MOUNTAINS". He looks
at ANNE while singing. Optional one minute of singing.

                    ANNE
          You used to bang on the dash, as if
          it was a bongo drum, while you sang
          that song.

                    TONY
          How did you know?

                    ANNE
          I know your whole life, Tony.

                    WOMAN #3
          Please sing "IF YOU FIND YOUR
          SWEETHEART IN THE ARMS OF A
          FRIEND". Okay?

                    TONY
          Sure. It doesn't make much sense,
          but as a song it's fun to sing.

TONY only looks specifically at ANNE when singing the lines:
"LOVE IS A THING, THAT YOU NEVER CAN SHARE". ANNE is close to
tears. Optional one minute of singing.

                    BILL
          How about singing that one again,
          Tony. At least three ladies here
          would appreciate it.

TONY repeats the song. After he finishes he offers his
handkerchief to ANNE. She uses it to wipe her tears.

                    LUCIENNE
          Are you okay, Anne?

                    ANNE
          I'm okay, in fact, I couldn't be
          better.

                    BILL
          Tony, what Western song would
          exactly show a family difference of
          philosophy - between your family
          and that of your former wife's?

                    TONY
               (singing)
          "I JUMPED FOR THE SADDLE AND THE
          SADDLE WEREN'T THERE - - AND I
          DROVE NINE INCHES UP THE OLD GREY
          MARE - - COME A TIE MY PECKER TO MY
          LEG, TO MY LEG - - COME A TIE MY
          PECKER TO MY LEG."

AD LIB and laughter from the group.

> TONY (CONT'D)
> They don't write them like that
> anymore!

AD LIB and laughter from the group.

> TONY (CONT'D)
> It's not a known fact, but the
> writer of that song was one of the
> founding fathers of the St. John's
> Ambulance Service.

AD LIB and laughter from the group.

> ANNE
> I haven't heard these songs for a
> lot of years.

> TONY
> You know them?

> ANNE
> No, I meant the way you sing them.
> I haven't heard you sing them for a
> lot of years.

> BILL
> Tony, did you ever have a pet,
> perhaps a dog?

> ANNE
> How about a girl friend's German
> Shepherd dog?

> TONY
> No, the only pet that I had was a
> horse in grade two. I had been
> living with my grandparents on a
> homestead. Unfortunately a very
> traumatic happening followed... He
> just bloated... He just kept
> getting bigger and bigger. Pretty
> soon it was like riding a mountain.

TONY pauses for effect, as he knows that the punch line
requires it. He takes a slow deliberate drink.

> WOMAN #1
> Well, what happened?

> TONY
> He got pregnant.

AD LIB and laughter from the group.

              BILL
He got pregnant?

              TONY
Well, when you're eight or nine
years old in that era, that is very
traumatic. Maybe you had to have
been there! Imagine some big stud
jumping up and down on your pet.
Especially when your horse is one
of the guys - your best buddy.

There is only polite laughter, due to this being a metaphor
related to ANNE.

              BILL
Tony, is there any song about a dog
to do with your first marriage?

              TONY
Yes. Bill, this is a song about my
first marriage and I would like to
dedicate it to my now dead poodle,
Coco. You may recognize it. It's an
old blues song from the thirties.

              BILL
I'm not that old, Tony.

              TONY
Did you have a dog in your
marriage, Bill?

              BILL
Yes, Tony. Her name was Lily.

              TONY
No Bill, not the tall dog, the
short one, the short one. Let's see
if you can name this song Bill.
It's about the dog that I miss from
my marriage.
                  (Tony repeats singing the
                  lines four times in a
                  blues fashion.)
I GOT A DOG WHO LOVES ME, AND A
WOMAN WHO SAYS SHE DON'T - I GOT A
DOG WHO LOVES ME, AND A WOMAN WHO
SAYS SHE WON'T.

              LORI
That was really bluesing it!

                    TONY
          Now Bill, can you guess the name of
          that song?

                    BILL
          "I GOT A DOG WHO LOVES ME, AND A
          WOMAN WHO SAYS SHE DON'T."

                    TONY
          No Bill, not the whole song!

Much laughter from the group.

                    ANNE
          I know Betty - at least I knew her -
          that's why I think this is so
          funny, Tony.

                    LORI
          What's your favorite breaking up
          song, Tony?

TONY then sings I WISH YOU LOVE - with the partial lines of:
YOU AND I CAN NEVER BE - - I WISH YOU LOVE. It is the only
song so far where TONY did not look at ANNE. Optional one
minute of singing.

                    TONY
          Man, I haven't sung that song in
          thirty years. It's too bad that all
          break ups can't be as civilized.

                    MAN #1
          How long have you been single?

                    TONY
          As of next year, exactly one-half
          of my adult life.

                    MAN #2
          I have to ask then. What's your
          favorite pick-up line?

TONY shakes his head in mock disbelief at the question.

                    TONY
          A drum roll please... My favorite
          pick-up line. I guarantee that it
          will produce results. You ask
          specifically: May I put it in once
          and if you don't like it, I promise
          I'll take it right out?

AD LIB and much laughter from the group.

                    TONY (CONT'D)
          I'm glad that I'm being ridiculous
          enough.

                    WOMAN #3
          If that's the best pick up line for
          a man, what's a great pick up line
          for a girl?

                    TONY
          Well, I know this is letting you
          know everything. So, here goes,
          it's: Would you like to stick it in
          just once, and if I don't really
          like it, you can take it out and
          have it back again.

AD LIB and much laughter from the group.

                    TONY (CONT'D)
          Don't try this at home.
               (looking at Anne)
          But, I guess most of you are single
          or unattached?

                    ANNE
          I'm definitely available... You
          know this is almost like when you
          used to tell your jokes at keg
          parties at Gull Lake.

                    TONY
          You remember that, you were there?

                    ANNE
          Yes Tony, I went to school with
          you.

                    TONY
          Were you bused in from a smaller
          country town?

                    ANNE
          No, I definitely lived in town and
          went to grade twelve with you. I
          was in your class.

                    MAN #1
          What was your favorite love song
          then, Tony?

ANNE moves to sit on a foot-stool near TONY.

                    ANNE
          You can sing it to me here.

                    TONY
          Um, to you? Okay.

TONY sings I ONLY HAVE EYES FOR YOU. ANNE is in a trance, as
he slowly looks at her face, her ears, her eyes and her
cheekbones. TONY has a puzzled look as usual, as he can't
figure out why he knows her so well. Two minutes of song.

                    ANNE
          Thank you, sir.

With short pauses for newly added ice and more Scotch, TONY
continues his singing. When he sings BLUEBERRY HILL, with its
lines of first love, TONY looks at ANNE with remembering
their first time together. TONY sings, WHAT NOW MY LOVE? He
gets one of the guys to beat the drums on the kitchen counter
for an emotional and rhythmic presentation of the song.
Optional one minute of singing.

                    TONY
          I'll now redeem myself, for those
          of you who may have not appreciated
          my jokes. One last song. As far as
          I know, it's the only song that
          Elvis Presley sang in Italian.

TONY sings SANTA LUCIA. He has memorized it by phonetics and
as such does not understand the words. LORI is busy talking
about her own Italian experiences through the first time of
singing the single verse, so TONY sings it three times for
all to hear. Optional two minutes of singing.

AD LIB and applause from the group.

                    LUCIENNE
          Wow... Wow! Bravo!

                    ANNE
          I want him!

LUCIENNE speaks to ANNE almost in mockery, loud enough such
that TONY can hear.

                    LUCIENNE
          Do you want him tonight? Don't
          forget your condition.

                    ANNE
          Always, I want him for always.

                    MAN #1
          So you remember everything from all
          of those eras throughout your life?
          Every song and style in detail?

                    TONY
               (Shrugs)
          I don't understand.

TONY walks across the room to fill his glass with Scotch and
ice. As he walked past LUCIENNE, she holds out her hand to
slow him down.

                    LUCIENNE
          Those are great songs from the
          past. It's too bad that you don't
          remember the people involved with
          you then. I know I'm also that way.
          I sometimes forget very important
          people in my life.

TONY smiles politely and completes his journey to pour
himself a drink. The crowd is dispersing. BILL makes a loud
remark as he is exiting.

                    BILL
          When I wake up tomorrow, I'll never
          believe that this singing and the
          jokes were a reality! Everything
          might be both timely and on target.

As others have disbursed Only ANNE, LORI and LUCIENNE are
left in the suite.

                    ANNE
          I guess the blondes have it
          tonight!

                    TONY
          You've changed your hairstyle! It's
          as if you had a nineteen-sixties
          hairstyle before.

                    ANNE
          We should definitely talk about
          that sometime... Maybe now?

                    TONY
          It was just a weird realization,
          that's all.

                    ANNE
Tony, there's something very
important and I don't want to leave
without saying it... Tony, I'm sure
that you don't know that you've
lost some of your memory. I'm also
very sure that you would like to
have your memory back.

                    TONY
Really? I guess I'm open to
suggestions.

                    ANNE
If you would cooperate with some
doctors, we can help you do that.
You won't be sorry, I promise.

                    TONY
Okay... I guess.

                    ANNE
You really did know me well, but
you've forgotten my entire family.
Yet you remember everything else.
It's as if I'm invisible. When we
do this, it's important that I
don't infer any former happenings,
nor influence your acquisition of
memory.

                    TONY
That's okay. You know, this is a
case of love at first sight, and I
guess the ease of loving someone
who reminds a person of a former
love. I trust you for that reason.

                    ANNE
We'll talk about a lot of things in
your past, with your thoughts being
the only thing important. We'll
slowly progress to grade twelve and
graduation. It may take a couple of
hours until you're ready to
remember our first summer of
intimacy. Okay?

                    TONY
Really? Sure, why not.

ANNE and TONY sit down on a sofa and begin to talk, just out
of sound range. DR. BILL joins them from having waited in the
hallway and sits across the small room on a chair.

Repeatedly, TONY states his condition of entering into what he now understands will be months of therapy.

                    DR. BILL
This process tonight will take
until about five a.m. Tony, you'll
be hypnotized to believe that you
got home at two a.m. Over a period
of months, your memory will slowly
return to you, all intact.

                    ANNE
We can keep on talking about a lot
in the past, Tony. But, tomorrow
you'll go back to forgetting that
we even met tonight - - just as you
usually would. You know, Tony, it
works because we were completely
candid with each other in the
distant past.

                    TONY
You know about my every sexual
involvement? Including homosexual
rape against me as a child? And
you're saying there are things that
I've forgotten? It doesn't seem
possible.

                    ANNE
You've now set aside every mental
anguish and anxiety that you ever
had. The doctors have said that
it's the ultimate of
rationalization. You simply accept
everybody.

                    TONY
How many times are you going to not
show up when I remember you? Or
dates of your supposed arrivals?

                    ANNE
A lot, I'm sorry. You'll see that
it'll work. I'll become real.

                    TONY
What about my thinking it's
confabulation. I've had a lot of
false memories in prior times.

DR. BILL
They were fill-in memories. When
you lost a group of memories, other
false memories took their place.
That's what true confabulation is.

TONY
Why won't I think that tonight was
confabulation?

DR. BILL
It will be a process of believing
in the optimistic thought patterns.
Is the glass half empty or is the
glass half full? If it's half empty
then you have false memories - -
and in your mind insanity. Half
full gives you reality and sanity.
It'll be your choice.

TONY
So eight months from now in
September, when I experience an
anxiety or fear of confabulation,
I'll do a counterbalance. Rather
than accept myself as having false
memories, I'll have to accept the
memories of Anne Thomson. That
might make sense, but I had eleven
shock treatments at a mental
hospital. It was all to do with
confabulation. I don't think that
you know what you're doing.

ANNE
I'm an outpatient from a mental
institution, Tony. I'm being
treated also. You can do it without
any other help. I know you can.

TONY
My memories hurt. They're like a
twisting in my stomach with a
knife.

ANNE
The therapy is slowly paced in
order to prevent any re-
traumatization. We can do it. We
can work on memories all the way up
to Christmas of 1964. You'll
remember it on your Christmas of
2003. In 1964 I attempted to say
good-bye.

                    DR. BILL
          The last programmed memories for
          you to bring back will be like a
          puzzle that you can completely put
          together on your own. Socially you
          will still have your normal friends
          and family.

                    TONY
          So, how do you have authorization
          for all of this?

                    DR. BILL
          I'm a registered psychiatrist. I
          also have a letter for you to sign.

TONY is handed the letter. He reads it and then begins to
write on it.

                    TONY
          I'll add a note about the unknown
          type of pill that you just gave me.
          Oh, and that I've drunk a portion
          of a bottle of Scotch.

                    DR. BILL
          I'll specify the type of pill, if
          you want.

TONY draws an engagement ring on the bottom right hand corner
of the letter.

                    TONY
          Are there any scissors available?

ANNE hands him small manicure scissors from her purse. TONY
cuts out a paper ring. ANNE sees what he has done.

                    ANNE
          Tony I would like to ask you to
          marry me. If you will, I will be
          your slave and your servant for the
          rest of our lives.

                    TONY
          Yes Anne. However, I need to add to
          your statement that I will honour
          you within a balance.

                    ANNE
          Tony will you marry me someday?

                    TONY
          Yes, Anne.

TONY pauses as he smiles at ANNE and he takes her left hand in his.

>   TONY (CONT'D)
>   I have a ring. Paper has
>   significance in anniversaries.
>   Perhaps it's not unusual for it to
>   have significance in engagements.
>   Two possibilities exist. One is
>   that this ring is in the same
>   category as a ring needing re-
>   sizing and can be replaced. The
>   other is that it has a weight and a
>   feeling of being around the finger.
>   Any of us that have worn a ring
>   know that's a tangible feeling.
>   Upon occasion if you put it on for
>   a minute, you'll be able to feel it
>   on your ring finger later.

>   ANNE
>   (with tears forming)
>   I love you Tony. I'll do both.

TONY tenderly places the paper ring on her finger. They kiss as the others stand wondering what part they should play. While simultaneously holding on to TONY with her right hand, ANNE displayed her left hand and the engagement ring in a manner fitting of any two-carat diamond. Her friends beam with pleasure. ANNE takes off her engagement ring and places it in one of the plastic photo holders in her wallet.

>   DISSOLVE TO:

EXT. BESIDE CAR ON THE STREET - THE NEXT NIGHT

LUCIENNE and TONY are standing outside of the Hot Jazz Club, a frequent haunt of Tony's. TONY has walked her to her car and she is about to get in.

>   LUCIENNE
>   That was a great time in there. I'm
>   glad that we all decided to meet
>   here after the party last night.
>   Only a couple of people couldn't
>   make it.

>   TONY
>   Yeah. It was fun.

>   LUCIENNE
>   One of the group that couldn't make
>   it was Anne. Do you remember her?

                    TONY
          No, I guess not.

                    LUCIENNE
          Well, she remembers you. She's
          going to leave her husband to be
          with you. Do you remember that?

                    TONY
          No. But I think that I remember all
          of the party. I don't forget
          drinking sessions.

                    LUCIENNE
          I have a bunch of questions. Can I
          ask them?

                    TONY
          Sure, why not.

                    LUCIENNE
          They'll seem kind of dumb.

                    TONY
          Go ahead.

                    LUCIENNE
          Here goes... Do you remember ever
          being hypnotized?

                    TONY
          Never.

                    LUCIENNE
          Do you think you were hypnotized at
          last night's party?

                    TONY
          For sure no.

                    LUCIENNE
          Do you remember a woman in Delta,
          that planned to leave her husband
          to be with you?

                    TONY
          I never went that far with anyone
          there.

                    LUCIENNE
          Not even a brunette that would stop
          by your house on certain occasions?

        TONY

No... No one did that. My wife was
a brunette.

        LUCIENNE

Do you know that you did the
equivalent of joining the French
Foreign Legion, when you went to
France the first time?

        TONY

Wow. That's really out there. No, I
didn't ever do that.

        LUCIENNE

Do you remember someone you were
very intimate with for a long
period of time, after high school?

        TONY

No, I never even went steady in
high school. There just wasn't
anyone who I liked that much. It
was a small town.

        LUCIENNE

Well, I know that the questions
seemed absurd. But so long for now,
Tony. I have to work early
tomorrow.

TONY and LUCIENNE kiss casually. LUCIENNE gets into the car
and waves as she drives off. TONY walks towards his own car
shaking his head at his perceived weirdness of it all.

                     CUT TO:

INT. A SPECIALTY COFFEE SHOP - DAY
CHARACTER #23
JAMES, REMARRIED, A LONG TERM FRIEND, HAS ALSO WORKED IN REAL
ESTATE SALES.

        JAMES

So you lost some of your memories
from years ago?

        TONY

I got them back.

        JAMES

What's this you were saying about
being hypnotized?

                    TONY
          Well, hypnosis is a tool... The
          power of it is with the patient.
          It's not like stage hypnosis. It's
          not even like psychotherapy, with
          insight-based stuff. Mostly it
          programs away the learned
          limitations like refusing to
          remember.

                    JAMES
          So, that's what you had? You called
          it Systemized Dissociative Amnesia?

                    TONY
          And that's a coping mechanism
          against trauma. It's often a memory
          loss about one specific family.
          Children often tend to dissociate
          when they're faced with abuse...
          And it can become a habit later
          until it causes confabulation.

JAMES looks up and shakes his head. He laughs.

                    JAMES
          And I thought you were normal.

                    TONY
          At least I now know who, what and
          where I was in 1964.

                                        CUT TO:

EXT. BESIDE A WHEAT FIELD, MID-WEST - DAY

TONY and ANNE are getting out of their convertible beside the
wheat field.

                    TONY
          Wait here a moment.

TONY walks into the center of the field. As a Straw Man he
stands with outstretched arms as he had done years before. He
stands facing away from ANNE. He then slowly turns around
with his arms still outstretched facing her. ANNE walks
toward him and as a Straw Woman she opens her arms in a
posture of being his balance as if in a ballet. They stand
for a moment, comprehending this metaphor. These were the
Straw People as a couple from a high school of so long ago.

They return to the edge of the field looking back to where
they had been. The Straw Man and Straw Woman are no more.

None of this has happened. The frame dissolves as to show
that this is a dream sequence. It was only his fantasy.

                                          DISSOLVE TO:

INT. GENERAL PRACTITIONER'S OFFICE (2004) - DAY

                    TONY
          It seems that I need to be referred
          to a psychiatrist... I have a new
          type of confabulation that I've
          never had before. I'm mostly here
          for the referral due to logic. In
          law it's called due diligence.

                    TONY'S DOCTOR
          I can give you some of the same
          medication as I gave you a number
          of years ago.

                    TONY
          I think it's worse than that. I'm
          sure that I've been hypnotized. For
          fourteen months now, I've been
          programmed by a supposed secret
          friend, so that I remember specific
          sequences of events. It may mimic
          schizophrenia.

                    TONY'S DOCTOR
          I'll make the referral and have
          them give you a call. Only a well-
          trained psychiatrist specializing
          in forensic psychiatry would be
          able to ascertain the reality, I
          have the name of one here.

                                          CUT TO:

INT. BEER GARDEN AT A JAZZ FESTIVAL, MUSIC PLAYS - DAY

                    TONY
          Hi, James. I haven't seen you
          around for awhile.

                    JAMES
          I like to get out now and them.

                    TONY
          Are you downtown for the day?

                    JAMES
No, I've just dropped in. You know,
home and family awaits.

                    TONY
Well I get a bit of a break these
days. Remember my offspring are a
few years older than yours.

                    JAMES
How did that first divorce go?

                    TONY
Let me be philosophical. Imagine a
straw man blowing in the wind. That
was me. I went through life proving
myself - - you know high family
standards. When we sold the five
thousand square foot home, I
realized that I didn't even want it
in the first place. I was catering
to a spoiled wife. I couldn't be
happier with my change.

                    JAMES
Tell me about it. I'm in that rut
now. If you don't mind me asking:
What is the main gain in you now
being single?

                    TONY
When I successfully petitioned for
a court order of maintenance
payments, I realize that I had
found a way to put a ceiling on
Betty's spending. I used a very
high figure, but for the first time
in almost two decades, I knew what
the figure was. It was an
incredible relief from pressure.

                    JAMES
You used to tell me what you were
spending. It must have been a
relief!

                    TONY
Initially after the separation, I
would walk down the street and I
couldn't help smiling. I walked
around grinning from ear to ear. I
had myself back again.

                    JAMES
          And the kids?

                    TONY
          I still see them as much as before.
          I lived only a couple of blocks
          away until Paul was sixteen. We're
          still very close. It's great!

The music increases in loudness and the two friends toast a
beer to each other.

                    JAMES
          And your second wife? What was her
          name, Lesley? Have you seen her
          lately?

                    TONY
               (shouting over the music)
          I still run into her at dances.
          She's returned to doing her
          fundamentalist thing. But when we
          broke up, it was more like two
          roommates going separate
          directions. I don't remember why we
          wanted to get married in the first
          place. She was pretty conniving and
          a narcissist. It seems like such a
          non-issue.

                    JAMES
          Did you understand her religion?

                    TONY
          Yeah, I've now studied Theology and
          the bible all of my adult life.
          That was the problem. Now I
          understand it. I'm not in awe of
          it.

                    JAMES
          Let's get together for a coffee
          next week.

                    TONY
          Got it - good idea.

TONY observes JAMES leaving the area, while JAMES is
nervously looking at his watch.

                                        CUT TO:

INT. A SMALL PSYCHIATRIST OFFICE - DAY

TONY is seated on an ordinary sofa, the doctor, PSYCHIATRIST #1, is behind a desk, just off screen.

>   PSYCHIATRIST #1 (O.S.)
>   You say that you believed you were
>   hypnotized for a reason? Tell me
>   about that reason.

>   TONY
>   I had confabulation a lot when I
>   was in my twenties. I overcame it
>   by writing everything down. I
>   literally never relied on my
>   memory, not even for simple
>   appointments.

>   PSYCHIATRIST #1 (O.S.)
>   And how does that affect you now?

>   TONY
>   The issue is that my memories are
>   returning. I now have a complete
>   autobiographical memory. I didn't
>   have them before. That tells me
>   that I've in effect been in therapy
>   and these people from the January
>   26th party existed.

>   PSYCHIATRIST #1 (O.S.)
>   Have you checked with anyone?

>   TONY
>   No, I've been afraid to.

>   PSYCHIATRIST #1 (O.S.)
>   Don't you think that you should
>   check now?

>   TONY
>   I guess it's time.

>   PSYCHIATRIST #1 (O.S.)
>   Memory distortions range from the
>   benign, like thinking that you
>   mailed a check, which you only
>   thought about mailing - to the
>   serious - to the fantastic like
>   claiming you piloted a spaceship.
>   We don't necessarily calibrate the
>   difference. Your problem isn't
>   really serious, not as long as you
>   get on with your life.

                    TONY
So this is just something to
ignore?

                    PSYCHIATRIST #1 (O.S.)
I think that confabulation created
your memory retrieval. Simple as
that.

                    TONY
So there is no Anne? She's just a
brunette that I met at a party?

                    PSYCHIATRIST #1 (O.S.)
Sometimes socially people say
things that can be misconstrued.

                    TONY
That would be impossible. I do
understand that memory is elusive
and that no two individuals can
perceive of a conversation the
same. The understanding of words,
with variances in culture and
education related to everything,
can vary. But saying that no
conversation existed about memory
retrieval - - seems way off.

                    PSYCHIATRIST #1 (O.S.)
Confabulation isn't uncommon. It's
simply the process of filling in
memory gaps by fabricating
information and details; done
either consciously or, as in the
case of amnesia, unconsciously. It
can be initiated by a post-
traumatic state as in the loss of a
loved one. At some point, you had
begun the amnesia process. It was
better than the pain of love. Also
memory disorders can result
following electroconvulsive
therapy, which unfortunately you
had.

                    TONY
I'll check out the party. I still
have the number of a couple of the
people that were there.

                                        DISSOLVE TO:

INT. TONY'S APARTMENT - NIGHT

TONY is sitting at his desk, he is alone.

INSERT: WITH AN EXTREME CLOSE UP OF TONY'S RÉSUMÉ. (HE READS
A SUMMARY OF IT OUT LOUD:) COMMERCIAL PROPERTY REALTOR FOR 14
YEARS - REAL ESTATE BROKERAGE MANAGER FOR 10 YEARS - PROPERTY
APPRAISER AND NEGOTIATOR FOR 7 YEARS. BACHELOR OF BUSINESS
ADMINISTRATION AND URBAN LAND ECONOMICS, MASTER OF BUSINESS
ADMINISTRATION IN DATA PROCESSING.

                    TONY
               (speaking out loud to
               himself)
          What a bunch of crap! It's not my
          profile. Where is the music, the
          creativity, the innovative
          processes, the love of cultures,
          the passions?

TONY stops in embarrassment, knowing that speaking to himself
is not what he wants to do. He continues in spite of himself.

                    TONY (CONT'D)
          Did she exist? Did she initiate the
          hypnotherapy? Did confabulation
          initiate the return of the
          memories? Are the memories valid?
          If so - why hasn't Anne shown up?
          It's been eighteen months.

TONY re-reads his information on hypnotherapy, out loud:

                    TONY (CONT'D)
          The journey is painful, but the
          rewards are great. The survivor can
          reclaim self-worth and rebuild life
          after so much focus on healing.
          There are often important life
          choices to be made about vocation
          and relationships at this time, as
          well as solidifying gains from
          treatment.

TONY yells with only the walls to hear him.

                    TONY (CONT'D)
          I'll paint, compose music, and
          write! I'll do it! Author, composer
          and artist! And I'll travel. My son
          is now a corporation. My daughter
          is married, has a career of her
          own. It's my turn!

Again TONY shows both embarrassment and confusion as related to talking to himself.

                                        CUT TO:

INT. SMALL PSYCHIATRIST'S OFFICE - DAY

TONY is again seated on the sofa, PSYCHIATRIST #1 is behind a desk. The desk is in view.

                    TONY
          I phoned Danielle, the blond from
          the January 26th party. She
          confirmed that she was there and
          that a number of flight attendants
          were also. She didn't know them.

                    PSYCHIATRIST #1 (O.S.)
          There you go. The scene is set. Now
          you know that it could have all
          happened in a multitude of ways.

                    TONY
          With my hurting memories, I moved
          from the victim stage, through the
          survivor stage, to the thriving
          stage. I'm where personal goals,
          not the trauma, have become a
          principle. The fact that this
          exists is irrelevant. It still
          seems to be orchestrated.

                    PSYCHIATRIST #1 (O.S.)
          When survivors can make sense of
          the trauma, they can better
          understand their reactions to it.
          You did that yourself.

                    TONY
          I did think that families or people
          from families were superior to me.
          I guess my roll has changed.

                    PSYCHIATRIST #1 (O.S.)
          It also sounds like you understand
          that religious zealots relative to
          their absurdity are not somehow
          above you in all things. That
          sounds like a big change in forty
          years. You know we don't have to
          analyze this. You're quite sane. I
          don't see anything irrational in
          your thoughts whatsoever.

                    TONY
          I guess that should to it. There
          was a bunch of other stuff that I
          read, such as secondary wounding
          and humiliation. All it said was
          that I had a right to manifesting
          post-traumatic stress disorder. I
          did a lot of other things, thrown
          in. Grief had to be dealt with. But
          I guess that I've reached the final
          stage of getting back the memories -
          simply accepting them.

                                        CUT TO:

EXT. MIDDLE OF A SMALL LAKE - DAY - FLASHBACK

ANNE and TONY are in a rowboat (1964).

                    TONY
          That was a beautiful evening, night
          and morning.

                    ANNE
          It was like a dream.

                    TONY
          We used to put up with being
          together on the front car seat so
          often. Having a real bed together
          was finally to be in our lives.

                    ANNE
          It's a beautiful day today. I'm
          looking forward to my life with
          Robert.

                    TONY
          What? That's a switch. What do you
          mean?

                    ANNE
          Everything is going the way it
          should, Tony.

                    TONY
          But, now we're not going to be
          together? What about us?

                    ANNE
        We'll see each other. You'll be
        successful... You can be with
        someone and even be at the same
        events as Robert and I. Just like
        our pastor said.

                    TONY
        That's not making any sense.

                    ANNE
                (smiling with glee)
        It's God's Plan! Our minister told
        us about the incredible opportunity
        that Robert and I will share as two
        children of the church!

                    TONY
        Did you just forget about what
        happened back there... In the
        cabin? Between us? Sexually?

                    ANNE
        When you put your life in the hands
        of God, many good things happen.

                    TONY
        God!

                    ANNE
        There is no choice, Tony. God has
        ways of punishing us if we leave
        our religious group. There need not
        be Armageddon! We are protected.

                    TONY
        Is that a cult?

                    ANNE
        It is love, Tony. Love for God and
        church. The evil works of Satan's
        demon have been driven from me.

                    TONY
        That's like you're two different
        people.

                    ANNE
        No, Tony. I've been saved by the
        Holy Spirit. Satan can't enter me.

                    TONY
        Can I talk to your minister?

                    ANNE
          No, Tony. You're not one of us. You
          don't want to pray like we do. You
          know I'm not afraid of the dark
          anymore?

                    TONY
          It's like mind control. It's a
          mental roller coaster ride. When my
          cousin studied at a Catholic
          seminary, we debated about sex
          before marriage. You used to agree
          with me... Not them.

                    ANNE
          That's why we say that we've seen
          the light.

                    TONY
          It makes me feel like a gigolo, a
          whore. We've now been enjoying sex
          together for years!

                    ANNE
          You're not a gigolo. Tony, you'll
          find somebody.

                                        DISSOLVE TO.

EXT. EDGE OF SMALL LAKE - MOMENTS LATER

TONY and ANNE are walking away from the boats at the dock.

                    TONY
          Did you enjoy that quick row-boat
          ride? It's too bad they didn't have
          motors.

                    ANNE
               (looking back, puzzled)
          It's as if I don't remember the
          boat ride. I guess I'm still in a
          daze from last night. I just
          remember everything after you
          carried me across the threshold.
          You vowed that it would be your
          only commitment in life. We had
          wonderful sex, Tony.

                    TONY
          It's starting to cloud over. Let's
          head back.

                              END OF FLASHBACK

INT. SECOND PSYCHIATRIST'S OFFICE - DAY (2005)

                    PSYCHIATRIST #2 (O.S.)
          How long have you had these
          memories?

                    TONY
          They just keep coming back. But the
          main thing is that I can't stop
          from thinking that Anne is
          arriving. I come up with dates, not
          consistently, but that center
          around things that are happening.

                    PSYCHIATRIST #2 (O.S.)
          Why not just think about something
          else?

                    TONY
          That's the point. She never stands
          me up. I always remember that she's
          not returning to meet with me...
          Just before the date. I then change
          it to another date. That's with
          focusing on new memories.

                    PSYCHIATRIST #2 (O.S.)
          But it didn't bother you for a few
          months. That's why you stopped
          seeing your former psychiatrist?

                    TONY
          Yeah, but he retired.

                    PSYCHIATRIST #2 (O.S.)
          What is it that I can do for you?
          What do you see happening?

                    TONY
          If it doesn't stop, then I'll
          commit myself to psychiatric care
          in a hospital. It's screwing up my
          life. I schedule everything around
          an arrival that never happens.

                    PSYCHIATRIST #2 (O.S.)
In our discussions here, I don't
hear anything erratic. Everyone has
something within their daily mental
process that isn't perfect.

                    TONY
Waiting for a former fiancée to
show up from almost forty years
ago, has to be unusual. When I made
this appointment, I was determined
to come up with a solution.

                    PSYCHIATRIST #2 (O.S.)
You mentioned due diligence. There
doesn't seem to be an issue of
anyone being in danger. When it
comes to thought patterns, the
world around us is very liberal.
You may go through decades of
waiting for a date to show up.
Others will just ignore the fact.

                    TONY
At the party, they said that it was
an issue of time. Neuron links have
to be redefined so that they become
operative. That takes time.

                    PSYCHIATRIST #2 (O.S.)
It's your choice. But, before I
discuss drug therapy, I'd like to
try something else. You may have a
form of Temporal Lobe Epilepsy.
It's a physical brain problem. This
is unlikely, however some of the
symptoms match. It takes a few
months to get in for an appointment
with a neurologist. And then it
will take about two months for the
analysis.

                    TONY
I'm after a solution to a problem
thing no matter what the outcome.

                    PSYCHIATRIST #2 (O.S.)
Usually individuals with Temporal
Lobe Epilepsy are argumentative.
Your willingness is probably the
first passing test.

                                    DISSOLVE TO:

INT. NEUROLOGIST'S OFFICE - DAY - ESTABLISHING

The room is shown to be the waiting room of a neurologist and
the time is shown on a wall clock, as the neurologist is one
hour late for his appointment. TONY is finally called in to
seem him as THE DOCTOR arrives with an armful of Christmas
gifts, showing the reason for the long wait.

INT. SECOND PSYCHIATRIST'S OFFICE - DAY (2005)

The PSYCHIATRIST is laughing and sharing Tony's joke.

                    PSYCHIATRIST #2 (O.S.)
         Sorry that it wasn't more painful.

                    TONY
         The entire time with the
         neurologist was less than an hour.
         He asked me redundant questions,
         checked my knee reflex with a small
         hammer, then told me I was okay.

                    PSYCHIATRIST #2 (O.S.)
         I now have to tell you, what to me
         is obvious. Your achievement of
         reconnecting with your memories of
         her is very possibly facilitated by
         the comfort level of believing in
         her consistent loyalty to you. It's
         confabulation for a purpose.

                    TONY
         I'm able to go through life without
         her. There are other real and alive
         women available.

                    PSYCHIATRIST #2 (O.S.)
         But, you quit doing it.

                    TONY
         I need to work on that.

                    PSYCHIATRIST #2 (O.S.)
         I'll prescribe Risperidone. They're
         pills that will relax and clear
         your mind. As with the drugs that
         you took when you were in your
         twenties, you need to watch for the
         side effects.

                    TONY
         I supposedly have a new date with
         Anne. It's the end of the month.

                    PSYCHIATRIST #2 (O.S.)
You may want to take the pills.

                    TONY
What about my change in life
styles? I now write, paint and
compose full time. This is more
probable than usual, given the
factor of Systemized Dissociative
Amnesia having been treated.
Apparently it rejuvenates people?

                    PSYCHIATRIST #2 (O.S.)
You are probably making rational
decisions. You're doing what you
always wanted to do. Unfortunately,
you're using an old girl friend as
a support system.

                    TONY
I made a list of all of my attempts
to replicate Anne. My relationships
have always been somewhat of a
duplication of my former big one.

                    PSYCHIATRIST #2 (O.S.)
That's logical, even if you didn't
have a conscious memory of her.

                    TONY
I remember their excuse, from the
January 2003 party. She's in a
mental institution. She's being
treated for D.I.D. Dissociative
Identity Disorder. Apparently the
treatment requires a number of
years.

                    PSYCHIATRIST #2 (O.S.)
It's a common scenario, that at our
age, we contemplate our
autobiographical portion of memory.
Most of the episodic memories are
true, even though they can be
inaccurate. To acquire those
missing portions by your efforts,
isn't unusual.

                    TONY
I'll take the pills.

                                        CUT TO:

INT. TONY'S APARTMENT - DAY (2006)

Tony's son, PAUL, is relaxed on his sofa.

                    PAUL
          I understand the amnesia, Dad. I
          studied it in psychology class. I
          guess we perspire so we're not too
          hot and similarly our minds protect
          us with memory loss.

                    TONY
          The amnesia in the past was a tip-
          of-the-tongue feeling. It was like
          I almost knew the family that I had
          forgotten. The greater the trauma,
          the greater the dissociation.

                    PAUL
          That's depressing. But, I guess
          it's not like lobotomies or shock
          treatments. It could be worse.

                    TONY
          No. I had simply gotten in the
          habit of setting aside emotions
          about anything traumatic when I was
          young, that was a type of amnesia.
          The hypnotherapy was based on the
          issue of the mind healing itself.
          It's just scheduled dates that I
          remembered. It's over now. Well
          pretty much.

                    PAUL
          That's good. You seem to be
          enjoying your life.

                    TONY
          Yeh. I thought that I'd also let
          you know about your Grandmother.
          You've obviously noticed that my
          patience level with her isn't that
          great. Now you know about my having
          grown up around pedophiles.

                    PAUL
          Just so you know that all
          homosexuals aren't pedophiles. Not
          any more than heterosexuals.

                    TONY
          Yeah, okay. I misspoke. My issue
          was with having to be around
          pedophiles. Anyway your Grandmother
          is a man hater. She's never got it
          together.

                    PAUL
          So where is the woman that you used
          to date?

                    TONY
               (unsure of himself)
          She's in a mental institution. She
          used fantasy instead of just
          forgetting.

                    PAUL
          Like I said, that's depressing.
          Anyway, let's go out for dinner.

                                        CUT TO:

INT. SECOND PSYCHIATRIST'S OFFICE - DAY

                    TONY
          So. I did a title search at the
          Land Title's office. They weren't
          owners then. So that was a dead
          end. I also searched in a
          crisscross directory. Nothing.

                    PSYCHIATRIST #2 (O.S.)
          Why did you think they would show
          up in documents?

                    TONY
          When I phoned Lucienne, she made
          the statement that she hadn't had a
          party. But when I phoned Danielle,
          she said that she had been there.
          So, my theory is more like a
          conspiracy theory. Lucienne was
          introducing the concept to me, that
          often people don't remember what
          they don't want to remember. I
          asked her if she knew a lady that I
          had gone to school with by the name
          of Anne Thomson or Davis and she
          said no. She was both polite and
          very convincing.

                    PSYCHIATRIST #2 (O.S.)
That is an ideal pattern. You need
to be sure one way or the other.

                    TONY
I wrote and outline down of what I
needed to do, as soon as she hung
up. A) The investigation of the
January 26, 2001 party, (B) an
autobiographical memory check, and
(C) finding Anne's phone number or
address. I'll head for our old high
school and in visiting I'll have
more information.

                    PSYCHIATRIST #2 (O.S.)
When have you visited last?

                    TONY
About thirty-five years ago. I'll
begin with looking at a yearbook
and our photograph. The one with
the heart.

                    PSYCHIATRIST #2 (O.S.)
Perhaps she's dead. It's been
awhile.

                    TONY
Danielle had said that there were a
lot of people there, most of them
from the airlines. As Anne worked
for the airlines, I think that she
was at the January 26 party.

                    PSYCHIATRIST #2 (O.S.)
Aren't you pursuing something that
is irrelevant to you?

                    TONY
I wrote a poem when I was in my
early twenties. It now makes sense
to me. It didn't before.
"MEMORIES:"
Memories are: gaieties, a cold
repose; trivialities, a hate warmed
froze; welcomed back, a sad affair;
a Cadillac, a get nowhere;
cherished thoughts, a hurting
thing; fun filled pots, a bad luck
bring; to the begotten,
to be forgotten - memories. - -
                    (MORE)

                        TONY (CONT'D)
        It was like a suicide note. Only
        instead of death, I might have
        forgotten everything... Everything
        about the Thomson family.

                        PSYCHIATRIST #2 (O.S.)
                (almost being sarcastic)
        Good luck.

                        TONY
        When I come back, I may need a lot
        of psychiatric help. I can only
        find out by visiting.

                        PSYCHIATRIST #2 (O.S.)
        Why would you need a lot of help?

                        TONY
        Because I may be completely off the
        deep end.

                                            CUT TO:

EXT. DRIVING AROUND A SMALL TOWN - DAY

M.O.S. TONY draws a diagram of each of the seven different
parking spots where he and ANNE had made love.

TONY does the same for each of his male friend's homes. Each
time that he drives up to the locations, he verifies that he
remembered correctly. He enthusiastically makes a large
positive check mark each time he is correct as nothing much
has changed in forty years.

INT. HIGH SCHOOL BUSINESS OFFICE - DAY - ESTABLISHING

TONY copies the photos from the yearbook that he needs. A
close up is shot of the photo of ANNE and TONY kissing.

INT. LOOKING OUT OF THE CAR WINDOW - DAY - ESTABLISHING

TONY drives by the "Drilling Mud" Warehouse. It has sunk at
least four feet with the ramp that had been level from a
boxcar to the warehouse floor level now having dropped down
at a forty-five degree angle. It is a vacant building, with
small broken windows.

INT. SMALL TOWN NEWSPAPER OFFICE - DAY

> TONY
> Could I see your microfiche
> archives, please?

> NEWSPAPER CLERK
> We don't use microfiche, but you
> can help yourself to all of the old
> newspapers. They're filed by dates
> going back to 1955.

> TONY
> Thanks, thanks a lot.

We see TONY focusing on a final photograph. It is of the new
elementary school teachers, showing ANNE and her cousin
DORIS, both having graduated the same year.

> TONY (CONT'D)
> (quietly to himself)
> I dated them both.

> CUT TO:

EXT. SMALL TOWN SIDEWALK - DAY - FLASHBACK

ANNE and a second male SCHOOL TEACHER from the group photo
are talking to TONY. (1964)

> ANNE
> Doris said that she gave you an
> ultimatum. Supposedly you need to
> get a university degree or enrol in
> a trade. She also told us the she
> had really put you in your place.
> She's become a real bitch, Tony.
> You need to drop her. Or she needs
> to figure out who she is.

TONY looks at another wedding photo. It's of ANNE THOMSON and
her new husband. TONY smiles, as if remembering each emotion.

> END OF FLASHBACK

EXT. MOTEL RESTAURANT - DAY - ESTABLISHING

TONY drives to Humber's Motel Restaurant, where he had dined
with GLORIA so long ago. As was now usual his prior diagrams
of the buildings and the parking lot were correct.

EXT. FARM FIELD - DAY - ESTABLISHING

TONY drives to the Federal Government Experimental farm where
the fields are now fenced. He is careful not to rip his
clothing as he goes through the wire. TONY holds his arms out
straight after reaching the center of the field and turns
slowly. It is muddy.

                                        DISSOLVE TO:

EXT. MOTEL ROOM - LATER

                    TONY
               (He takes a deep breath
                and phones.)
          Hello. Is this Anne Dean?

                    ANNE
          Yes. It is. May I help you?

                    TONY
          Yes. My name is Tony... I don't
          know if you remember me. You were
          Anne Thomson, I believe.

                    ANNE
          Yes, I was. Yes, I do remember you.

                    TONY
          I thought that I would give you and
          David a call as I was in town just
          for the day. I believe we dated if
          I remember correctly. It was a lot
          of years ago.

                    ANNE
          I haven't heard from you or about
          you in a lot of years! We were
          definitely in the same crowd. We
          all hung out together - with
          Richard Berry and all of the
          others. I do certainly remember
          you. We did everything together. I
          don't know if we dated. We went to
          quite a few dances. I remember that
          we always danced together.

                    TONY
          That's how I remember it. I was
          always going to give a phone call
          when I came through. I haven't been
          back for a lot of years.

                    ANNE
Are you going to be here at the
high school reunion in June?

                    TONY
I don't actually know about it.

                    ANNE
Oh, it's good you called then. It
would be wonderful if our old gang
were together again! I believe that
it's June 13th, 14th, and 15th. I
have so much stuff here on it. I
don't know if I can even find the
date in it. But I do have a number
for you to call for information.

                    TONY
Great. That would be ideal.

                    ANNE
One of the nights is to be catered
with Lobster being brought in. I
know they've gone to a lot of work
looking after details.

                    TONY
That sounds great. I'll probably be
here.

                    ANNE
So, what have you been up to?

                    TONY
I was in real estate as an
appraiser and property negotiator
for years - in Vancouver, where I
live. Last fall I semi-retired - or
maybe it was more like a change in
careers. Presently I write and
paint. It's involvement in the
arts.

                    ANNE
It will be really good to see you
again. If you're semi-retired you
will definitely have time off to
come. You're probably the furthest
of our bunch for travelling time.

                    TONY
          Our photo was in the yearbook
          together and I thought I should say
          hello. I couldn't remember the
          details.

                    ANNE
          I'm glad you did. It's always
          really great to be in touch with
          the old crowd.

ANNE gives him the contact number in a very assuming manner,
with the voice of an old friend.

                    TONY
          Thanks. I'll phone him. You were a
          schoolteacher, were you not? It
          seems to me that was your plan.

                    ANNE
          Yes. This is the first year that
          I've been home in all of those
          years. Now it's just grandchildren
          and that sort of thing. Nothing
          much else, but it keeps me busy.
          The days fly by though.

                    TONY
          I look forward to seeing you folks
          next month.

                    ANNE
          Me too! David will be home shortly.
          He's at work. It's been really
          nice to talk to you again, Tony.

                    TONY
          Thanks. I'll give William a call
          for the information. Good-bye.

                    ANNE
          Good-bye, Tony.

TONY quickly wrote down a summary of their conversation as if
knowing that he would be needing to read it many times.

                                        CUT TO:

INT. SECOND PSYCHIATRIST'S OFFICE - DAY

                    TONY
               (smiling very happily)
          My high school town was more than a
          little taken care of... But I can't
          believe what I found!
               (MORE)

                    TONY (CONT'D)
I had the wrong girl. This wasn't
about Anne Thomson - it was about
her cousin, Doris Snyder - the love
of my life, Doris Snyder.

                    PSYCHIATRIST #2 (O.S.)
I have to ask... Are you taking
your pills?

                    TONY
It was the church lady and little
girl face, of Doris, which was
typically one of a scowl. It was
that expression, which was shown in
the group photo. That was unique
enough to motivate me to remember
that, in fact, I had been the
fiancée of Doris, not Anne.

                    PSYCHIATRIST #2 (O.S.)
Your memories all came together and
made sense at that point?

                    TONY
Yes.

                    PSYCHIATRIST #2 (O.S.)
If it makes sense to you then you
don't have a problem.

                    TONY
      (excited)
Actually, I never started taking
the pills. I'm really becoming sure
of this. I'm so sure that I now
understand a second poem. I thought
that it was about my mother. It
wasn't. It was about a young lady
who reminded me of my mother.

                    PSYCHIATRIST #2 (O.S.)
Is that important to you?

                    TONY
              (speaking firmly)
It was about finally understanding
Doris. "ENFIN:"
What hold hath she that calleth to
thee, my frightful friend to the
end, whilst not godsend?
What spirit tis this?
Tis no wonderis bliss?
Who calls through the day and in
the night doth stay far away?
Who darith demand both thy hand
and yet prevails to backward wails?
Who is this fright
this awful might?
This door ajar from near yet far?
What is this roar
this lowest whore,
never true, forever blue?
Your Mother? - -
For years I thought it was
different. I had forgotten why I
put a question mark at the end. It
meant, "like your mother".

                PSYCHIATRIST #2 (O.S.)
Are you coping with your life on a
daily basis?

                    TONY
I'm working at my chosen avocation,
living where I want and enjoying
both my son's and daughter's
reactions to life... The single's
scene in general can now be my
focus. It's all good.

                PSYCHIATRIST #2 (O.S.)
Are all of your memories distorted?
That is when you remembered Anne in
your past, it was really always
Doris?

                    TONY
Yes. Anne was only a friend. Doris
was the one that I had the long
term relationship with. And...
Doris was the one that was in Delta
and a part of my life later.

                    PSYCHIATRIST #2 (O.S.)
          You mentioned that some memories
          are more traumatic or major than
          others. What is an example of a
          major memory.

TONY looks up at the ceiling and slowly shakes his head to
the negative.

                                        CUT TO:

EXT. CITY PARK JOGGING TRAIL (1963) - DAY - FLASHBACK
CHARACTER #24
DORIS LOOKS LIKE HER COUSIN, ANNE. THEIR RESEMBLANCE IS
THOUGHT OF AS LIKE SISTERS. THE DIFFERENCE IS THAT DORIS
OFTEN WEARS HER HAIR IN WHAT WILL BE KNOWN AS THE STYLE OF A
CHURCH LADY, ALONG WITH DRESSING AS SUCH. AS SHE HAS THREE
DISTINCT ERRATIC PERSONALITIES, WITHOUT MEMORY BETWEEN THEM,
SHE IS SUBTLY SHOWN WITH THREE DIFFERENT FACIAL EXPRESSIONS.

                    TONY
          It just seems that I went to
          technical school to please my
          relatives. I saw everything through
          a filter that was about their life.
          It wasn't really what I want to do.
          Are you saying that you became an
          elementary school teacher for the
          same reason?

                    DORIS
               (as her intelligent self)
          Tony, just that fact that we both
          exercise with jogging, should tell
          us how different we are from our
          relatives. Now that we're living
          together, we get to experience the
          contemporary world. It's our life,
          not theirs.

                    TONY
          You were going to tell me about a
          thought you had to do with work.

                    DORIS
          You know, when we talked about
          pursuing an educated life, we
          always included teaching elementary
          school. But, I think I've been
          taken advantage of.

                    TONY
          I think I get it.

                    DORIS
          What my teaching certificate has
          allowed me to do is to be trapped
          into helping grade-three students
          color posters for the rest of my
          life.

                    TONY
          That's hardly philosophy or
          culture. That's what you used to
          want.

                    DORIS
          I know. I want to do what you want
          to do. Travel - acquire an
          understanding of the world -
          experience other cultures.

                    TONY
          We can do that. Now we can plan
          together. Starting this summer we
          can work towards new goals.

                                   DISSOLVE TO:

INT. TONY'S AND DORIS'S APARTMENT, NEXT DAY - DAY - FLASHBACK

                    DORIS
          I just remembered. I promised to go
          to a Country and Western concert
          with Jacob Wagner tonight. He
          purchased front row tickets about
          two months ago.

                    TONY
          You don't have to go with him. I
          can buy them from him.

                    DORIS
          No. He's an old school friend and
          our relationship has always been
          platonic. My sister Phyllis is
          coming over this afternoon - so you
          can visit with her.

M.O.S. DORIS goes into the bedroom and stays for two hours.
PHYLLIS, arrives and she and TONY visit. AD LIB also M.O.S.

DORIS comes out of the bedroom only long enough to take two
pieces of ordered-in chicken back with her. She slams the
bedroom door showing that she is distant to TONY whereas only
nine hours before she had been melting in an embrace. DORIS
comes out of the bedroom about seven o'clock.

                    PHYLLIS
          Doris purchased the black dress for
          a special occasion with you, Tony.
          She's about to show it off.

TONY goes over to DORIS to give her a kiss.

                    TONY
          That's a beautiful dress. You look
          very cute.

                    DORIS
          Don't call me cute!

DORIS crosses her arms with the scowl often shown with this
personality. She leans back against the wall.

                    DORIS (CONT'D)
          And I'm not about to neck with you
          and go out with someone else.

DORIS looks out the window and sees JACOB outside. She leaves
to join him in an excited fashion.

                                        DISSOLVE TO:

INT. TONY'S AND DORIS'S APARTMENT - LATER - FLASHBACK

PHYLLIS, looks nervously at her watch. TONY and her keep
visiting, however, both know that something is terribly
wrong. They hear DORIS and JACOB at the door. DORIS is
laughing very loudly as she enters the room by herself. TONY
stands up in welcoming her.

                    DORIS
          I've already had one date tonight -
          I don't need another! Leave
          immediately Tony. I can't see how
          you can stay over, given the
          circumstances.

                    TONY
               (politely, trying to
                accommodate)
          Okay, I'll come back tomorrow.

                    DORIS
          No. Jacob and I are going to a
          Billy Graham Evangelical Service.

DORIS goes into their bedroom shouting:

                    DORIS (CONT'D)
Get him out of here. He's stalking
me. I have a right to date!

                    TONY
Are you sure you mean that? I can
stay at the work site.

                    DORIS
Jacob said that he noticed that you
and Phyllis - sure did get along
and think alike. You would make a
good couple.

                    PHYLLIS
If this is her idea of dating in
the sixties, I don't want any part
of it! It's not fair, Tony!

                    TONY
We were so intimate last night. But
now its like she has forgotten that
I live here.

                    PHYLLIS
She's going through something that
we don't understand. I really
don't. She loves you. She raves
about you two being together.
Someday we'll figure it out.

                                    END FLASHBACK

INT. SECOND PSYCHIATRIST'S OFFICE - DAY

                    TONY
I guess that with all of my
memories, it all seems so normal.
That is my not remembering seems
normal.

                    PSYCHIATRIST #2 (O.S.)
Is there more? Do you have, say,
one other?

                    TONY
Turville and me being blamed for
rape.

                    PSYCHIATRIST #2 (O.S.)
That sounds eventful.

                    TONY
          As if to confirm that it was okay
          to have such thoughts, I kept
          reflecting on a small country and
          western dance. Just before leaving
          for France, Doris had phoned for
          yet another last evening together.
          She wanted me to accept her new
          community. On the way she asked me
          to sing a few hillbilly songs.

INT. ONE ROOM SCHOOLHOUSE - NIGHT - FLASHBACK

Students' desks are stacked around the perimeter of the
single room. A local country BAND is starting to play, with
the DRUMMER late as usual.

DORIS is dancing close to TONY as her normal personality.

                    DORIS
          I don't know why I thought I should
          marry Jacob. It's now us, Tony.
          Only us.

TONY and DORIS dance as close as a couple could physically be
in public.

                    TONY
          Does this make sense, to keep
          changing your mind?

                    DORIS
          I know my mind and here in your
          arms is what matters. Tony you're
          it. I should have known it before.

M.O.S. They jive, waltz and laugh. CAROL, three years older,
is an old friend, who visits with them along with her new
husband. They joke as a foursome would on a dance floor.

Intermission for the band is announced.

                    DORIS (CONT'D)
          I'll just go to the powder room and
          then we can go, Tony. I feel so
          much better now.

As DORIS walks away she wears the happy look of a woman in
love. DORIS returns with a scowled expression. She has been
crying. She rejects Tony's hand around her waist in exiting.

                                        DISSOLVE TO:

EXT. OUTSIDE SCHOOLHOUSE - NIGHT - FLASHBACK

Walking to the car, TONY reaches over to take her hand. DORIS jerks her hand away as if pouting and then walks ahead of him.

As the snow is piled up on the car passenger side, TONY opens his door and she slides in.

TONY turns on the car and waits for the heater to kick in. Simultaneously he puts his arm around her. Due to years of intimacy he slides his left hand onto her right side, lightly touching the side of her breast.

DORIS swings at him, not connecting. She opens her door, forcing it against the snow bank and runs down the road.

In his rear view mirror TONY observes this and her then talking to two individuals near their car. He sees a man running towards him.

TONY steps out of his car as the man hits him in the jaw.

>   THE MAN FROM THE CAR
>   You bastard! You want to rape an
>   innocent girl? I'll show you what
>   force will do.

He swings and connects with TONY'S left ear.

>   TONY
>   What are you talking about? We're
>   engaged.

CAROL, one of the two individuals, runs up to them.

>   CAROL
>   Stop! There's been a mistake. This
>   is Tony and Doris! Something's
>   wrong that we don't know about.
>   Just wait here with Tony. I'll find
>   out what it is. It's like mother,
>   you know. It's like my
>   schizophrenic mother. I'll be right
>   back.

The two men lean on Tony's car, neither knowing what might be said. They wait. CAROL almost immediately runs back to them. She is out of breath.

>   CAROL (CONT'D)
>   Doris wants a ride to her old town
>   of Alex. But I know that she
>   doesn't live there anymore.
>   (MORE)

                    CAROL (CONT'D)
She also thought that I'm her
teacher. But, we worked together in
both student teaching and as
substitute teachers.

                    TONY
She thinks she's a grade school
student? I need to talk to her.

                    CAROL
No Tony. You know my brother well
and you probably know about my
mother. She's spent half of her
life in a mental institution. We
can talk tomorrow by phone. We'll
take care of her.

                                END FLASHBACK

INT. SECOND PSYCHIATRIST'S OFFICE - DAY

The face of the PSYCHIATRIST #2 is shown for the first time,
as symbolic of clarity and reality being easier for TONY.

                    TONY
I spoke twice with Carol over the
next few days. I let her know that
I was headed for Europe and she was
one person who really agreed with
my logic.

                    PSYCHIATRIST #2
That was the last time you heard
from Doris?

                    TONY
When I got back from Europe I heard
of me being accused of rape of a
sort. Later Doris changed her
story. Most people just laughed.

                    PSYCHIATRIST #2
Did you feel responsible?

                    TONY
Yes, in some way. But I should have
remembered Turville. Everything
would have made sense. I would
have known - I wasn't the bad guy.

                    PSYCHIATRIST #2
It may never make sense.

INT: A HIGH RISE APARTMENT, THROUGH THE WINDOW OF TONY'S CAR –
ESTABLISHING

TONY drives by their former apartment home. He stops and
looks through his front car window. He shakes his head as
someone deep in thought. It is in present time.

CUT TO:

INT. HOSPITAL ROOM - NIGHT

TONY is sitting in a chair next to the bed. HIS MOTHER, now
elderly is mid-eighties and is very thin from lung cancer and
she waivers in and out of sleep.

> TONY
> (in a low voice)
> You know Mom, you've moved from
> Delta now and we can think about
> our past in all those other little
> towns on the prairies... We've been
> through a lot together with our
> lives being so entwined - and you
> know - in spite of everything,
> we've come out okay.
> (he smiles)
> Forgiveness... It's acceptance with
> no need to hate. I accept you as
> you simply being what you are. My
> memories no longer hurt. I was a
> victim and I wasn't responsible.

TONY'S MOTHER smiles weakly.

CUT TO:

INT. APARTMENT (2008) - NIGHT

A gathering with others including, as on January 26, 2003:
DORIS, LUCIENNE, LORI, DR. BILL, JOHN, DANIELLE, and TONY.

AD LIB from the group as background.

> DORIS
> (speaking to Lucienne)
> Yes, you only had to send one
> invitation. I do only have one
> personality now.

> LUCIENNE
> No, I meant are you living
> together?

                    DORIS
As sanity would have it, yes.

                    TONY
Neither one of us has memory
problems anymore. That's very cool.

                    LUCIENNE
What was the hardest thing to
accept, Tony.

                    TONY
For me, it was that the memories
were real. For Doris, it was that
she couldn't remember actions and
words from the times of her other
personalities. I also couldn't
accept the period of time that it
took for our memory to normalize.

                    LORI
How long was that?

                    TONY
Over five years for me was needed.
We used ten. Longer for Doris.

                    LUCIENNE
Did you ever contact Anne?

                    TONY
Doris and I met with her to thank
her. But no, I actually never
approached her during the process.

                    DR. BILL
It's over. You now have a clear
past, therefore a clear present and
a clearly planned future. What do
you do now?

                    TONY
Live happy ever after - with loves
truly born again - Becky by any
other name, is BECKY. With memory,
I also can know who Becky is! And
of course I now understand that I
may have never been a straw man if
I had held all of my memory
throughout my life. I really am my
own person now!

                    LORI
Was it worth it? That was a lot of
time... even for having to remember
Doris as Anne.

                    TONY
I'm now able to make decisions
without emotional prejudice
involving a use of half-memories.

                    DORIS
His inner conscience no longer
controls with a set of rules
completely unknown to Tony.

                    TONY
          (smiling)
True and my present pride has
replaced my former shame of my
growing-up years. I'm going through
life with the usual reflections -
the smiles or remembering, to do
with a life well lived.

                    DR. BILL
Many people should review their
life as you have, as a great
exercise. When survivors can make
sense of the trauma, they can
better understand their reactions
to it. You did that yourself.

                    TONY
          (laughing)
You're biased Bill. I really do
have other things to do now! But I
really did think that those
families were superior to me. My
review of it all was with a
different perception.

                    LORI
          (lifting up her wine
           glass)
Well I'm here to propose a toast.
To memory!

The others all join in with lifting their glasses.

                    TONY
To memory!

                                        DISSOLVE TO:

EXT. AIRPORT PASSENGER DROP OFF AREA - DAY

Noise of the busy airport terminal is in the background. TONY
and DORIS are standing facing each other. Tony's suitcases
are at his sides.

>   TONY
>   Thanks for driving me to the
>   airport, Doris.

>   DORIS
>   I really both hated and wanted to,
>   Tony. You need your life as you
>   define it.

>   TONY
>   I now have my life.

>   DORIS
>   As the Phoenix flies towards the
>   sun and the planets, and towards
>   all that may be promised to a man.
>   You said that once!

TONY kisses her cheek tenderly.

>   TONY
>   I do enjoy an international bent to
>   my life now.

>   DORIS
>   Bye Tony. I'll always remember you.

>   TONY
>   Bye Doris. I'll never forget you.
>   Thanks. Bye.

A very spry but older TONY turns and walks away with
suitcases in hand. Doris's car is shown to be driving away.
Tony's plane is shown taking off into the sky.
FREEZE FRAME
TEXT OVER SCREEN:
THE AUTHOR, BEING THE PROTAGONIST, ENJOYED INTERNATIONAL
TRAVEL, WORLD MUSIC AND OTHER RELATIONSHIPS THROUGHOUT THE
LAST YEARS OF THE HYPNOTHERAPY PROCESS. HE NOW HAS HIS FULL
MEMORY.

>   FADE OUT.
>   THE END

www.ingramcontent.com/pod-product-compliance
Lightning Source LLC
Chambersburg PA
CBHW081657270326
41933CB00017B/3202